Women of Courage

Also by Debra Evans

Women *of* Courage

INSPIRING STORIES *of* FAITH, HOPE, AND ENDURANCE

DEBRA EVANS

ZondervanPublishingHouse
Grand Rapids, Michigan

A Division of HarperCollinsPublishers

Women of Courage
Copyright © 1999 by Debra Evans

Requests for information should be addressed to:

📖 ZondervanPublishingHouse
Grand Rapids, Michigan 49530

Library of Congress Cataloging-in-Publication Data

Evans, Debra.
    Women of Courage : inspiring stories of faith, hope, and endurance / Debra
Evans.
       p.   cm.
    Includes bibliographical references.
    ISBN 0-310-23837-4 (Softcover)
    1. Christian women—Religious life.   2. Women in the Bible—Biography.
3. Christian women—Biography.   I. Title.
BV4527.E894 1999
248.8'43—dc21   99-18859

                                                  CIP

Published in association with Wolgemuth and Associates, Inc., 8600 Crestgate Circle,
Orlando, FL 32819.

Interior design by Sherri Hoffman
Printed in the United States of America

00 01 02 03 04 05 06 /❖ DC/ 10 9 8 7 6 5 4 3 2 1

For Abigail

Contents

Acknowledgments

These are the people I especially want to thank for their advice, understanding, prayers, and support during the past year: my amazing senior editor, Sandra Vander Zicht; my trustworthy literary agent, Jennifer Cortez; my parents, John and Nancy Munger; my sisters, Kerry Olson and Nancy Shallow; my children, Joanna White and Katherine, David, and Jon Evans; and my husband, David. Your between-the-lines participation in the writing of this book helped create and fill its pages.

So do not fear, for I am
    with you; do not be dismayed,
    for I am your God.
I will strengthen you
    and help you;
I will uphold you with my
    righteous right hand.

—Isaiah 41:10

Introduction

Our God meets us just where we are. But He does not leave us there. There is power in the word of a King to effect what it commands. In the Fear not of our God, repeated from Genesis to Revelation, there is power to give us just what we lack at that moment.[1]

— Amy Carmichael (1867–1951)

Being constantly courageous, at least in Christian terms, doesn't mean being tough. It means being tender toward God and his purposes. The lives of the saints — those with the title before their names and those with no appellation — strangely and wonderfully demonstrate that Christian "courageousness" means being Jesus' true friend. Through their stories we see and understand: God alone supplies the strength, the glory, the light by which the next step is revealed; he delivers peace and rest when the terrain appears unnavigable; his presence is spiritual protection, granitelike in its ability to withstand every enemy attack.

This book tells the stories of twelve women whose lives and faith give us memorable examples of godly courage. As you read their stories, recognize their struggles, and imagine their victories, I trust you will be encouraged by their lasting witness.

The Bible reminds us that we are indeed surrounded by "a great cloud of witnesses" (Heb. 12:1) from whom we are to gain encouragement as we run toward the finish line of our faith. In his book *The Fight,* Christian psychiatrist John White invites us to picture the splendid scene this way:

11

"Moses is at your elbow as you approach the starting point. So are Joshua and Rahab the harlot. So, too, are thousands of unknowns who went through hell on earth and proved God true. They are straining to speak to you, to tell you something; and about someone."[2]

Women of Courage was written to link this rich legacy from the past with our lives today. The testimonies of courageous women, from Hagar of the Genesis era to contemporary Rosa Parks, teach us about God's power, about God's love for us, and about our dependence on him.

"Blessed are the poor in spirit, for theirs is the kingdom of heaven" (Matt. 5:3). I see this, the starting point for Jesus' Sermon on the Mount, as the starting point for *Women of Courage.* I've spent months studying, researching, and contemplating the lives of valiant women in church history who stood firm and walked tall, displaying great courage. And this is what I've learned: Great courage requires true surrender. Their bravery could not have been self-created on the spur of the moment; it clearly came from Christ — their defender, protector, counselor, guide, and friend — as they looked to him for strength in faith, with love.

Eugene Peterson notes, "Christian faith is not neurotic dependency, but childlike trust. We do not have a God who forever indulges our whims, but a God whom we trust with our destinies. The Christian is not a naive, innocent infant who has no identity apart from a feeling of being comforted and protected and catered to, but a person who has discovered an identity that is given by God, which can be enjoyed best and fully in a voluntary trust in God. We do not cling to God desperately out of fear and the panic of insecurity; we come to him freely in faith and love."[3]

Still, our tendency, given the limits of our self-determining "me first" nature, is to try to prove to God (and others) that we are capable, wise, and courageous without him. What a shocking disappointment it is when we hit our first major obstacle and fall crashing to the ground! After the tenth time, we may begin to get a hint. By the fiftieth, we probably start paying attention. By the thousandth time, we finally might be on the verge of developing real Christian humility, realizing that God is our strength, our help in trouble.

That's why we need to consider the women who have gone before us whose faith has fueled their courage. Through their witness, they show us why standing still is sometimes more important than moving ahead. They teach us about the value of listening, waiting, and observing. We gain confidence as we draw near to their solitary experience with God and are encouraged to spend more time with Jesus.

This book, *Women of Courage*, like my previous companion book, *Women of Character*, is designed to help you draw upon the valuable resources that are ours through our rich heritage. In writing, I've drawn upon biblical accounts of valiant women who put their faith in God; writings by and about women of faith from the early days of the church until now; classical literature, including hymns and poems, expressing facets of the Christian experience; the rich treasury of the Psalms, the Prophets, and the Epistles; and devotional literature from more recent times.

Each chapter has a central theme to consider as you read and study. At the heart of each chapter is the story of a woman from Scripture whose life illuminates the topic. Then a second woman's story comes from church history. Introductory and concluding discussions include personal comments from contemporary Christian women. I've also chosen pertinent quotations from the Scriptures and from other sources, open-ended questions to prompt personal reflection and/or group discussion, Bible study, and prayers for your enjoyment and encouragement.

As you sort through the eclectic life patterns presented here, you might want to keep a journal. Perhaps the poems, prayers, hymns, and psalms will inspire you to creatively express to the Lord your own thoughts and reactions. Don't worry about any flaws that may turn up in your handiwork. Your honest, heartfelt efforts will produce something beautiful for God.

As I look into the lives of women who went before me, I see the image and character of God reflected in their brave, trusting hearts — women who were willing to grow up into their full stature as the saints we are *all* becoming. It is as if, by their radiant witness, they are vigorously inviting each of us to let go of our fear and doubt as we face a future that is unknown to us, but not to our God.

Chapter One

❧

By Faith

It is the easiest thing in the world to obey God when He commands us to do what we like, and to trust Him when the path is all sunshine. The real victory of faith is to trust God in the dark, and through the dark.[1]

— Theodore L. Cuyler (1822–1909)

Trusting God in the dark — and through the dark — doesn't make sense from a purely rational standpoint. Darkness provokes distrust, disorientation, and a troubling sense that all is not as it should be.

Sheila Walsh says that courage is not the absence of fear. Rather, for a Christian, courage and fear are "strange bedmates. . . . Fear tells us that life is unpredictable, anything can happen; courage replies quietly, 'Yes, but God is in control.'"[2]

Think of your life and your life's journey. When you're "walking in the dark," where do you look to discover which way to go? What do you trust? Whom do you trust? I turn first to some Scriptures I've learned, and I draw from my memory: "Trust in the Lord with all your heart and lean not on your own understanding" (Prov. 3:5). I remember Jesus' words to his disciples: "Do not let your hearts be troubled. Trust in God; trust also in me" (John 14:1). And the apostle Paul's blessing to Rome's earliest Christians: "May the God of hope fill you with all joy and peace as you trust in him, so that you may overflow with hope by the power of the Holy Spirit" (Rom. 15:13).

These memorable words help me get my bearings when I'm walking in the dark, when fear and doubt come creeping onto my path, into my heart. Thankfully, trust doesn't depend on our sensory perceptions for validation. Trust isn't about positive feelings — it's about childlike faith.

The writer of the epistle to the first Jewish Christians rhetorically asked, "What is faith?" The answer? "It is the confident assurance that what we hope for is going to happen. It is the evidence of things we cannot yet see" (Heb. 11:1 NLB). In a similar way, the apostle Paul describes another virtue often connected to faith — hope: "Hope that is seen is no hope at all. Who hopes for what he already has?" (Rom. 8:24).

Faith ... hope ... trust. How willing are we to walk into unfamiliar territory, into a place where God requires us to rely on him alone? To go where our Shepherd leads, even when we can't make any sense out of our surroundings? To follow Jesus with childlike trust?

If you have read *Women of Character*, you may remember the story of the birth of my granddaughter Abigail. We didn't know in advance that Abigail would arrive with multiple challenges to her central nervous system or that she would have a critical need for immediate surgery — an operation to close a small opening in her back caused by a disabling developmental condition called spina bifida. We didn't know what the future would hold for Abigail: How many more surgeries would she need? When would she be able to walk? To what degree would her condition affect her growth, her learning rate, her life expectancy? Abigail is now five years old, and we still don't know the answers to those questions. None of us can see that far ahead.

Being Abigail's grandmother has brought me new lessons in faith, in hope, in trust in God. I've learned something about the kinds of questions I ask: questions more concerned with today than with tomorrow, more concerned with who she is than with what she can and cannot do. When I'm with her, my thoughts ordinarily center on Abigail — whatever she may be feeling, thinking, doing, and saying — rather than on the myriad hopes and concerns I have regarding her future. Because Abigail's development is quite unpredictable, I avoid making predictions. This helps me to focus on my granddaughter instead of on my own expectations.

From Abigail I'm learning about a childlike trust in God. When I look into Abigail's bright blue eyes, she is usually very eager to engage my full attention. Her trust in God is wonderfully uncomplicated. She has already figured out many of life's most important fundamental things and surprises me with the depth of her spiritual understanding.

Abigail's acceptance of Christ came about simply, as it does for so many children, without any apparent struggle or debate. One night, when my daughter Joanna was tucking Abigail in bed, Abigail looked into her mom's eyes and pointed to her own heart.

"What is it, Abigail?" Joanna asked.

"Jesus . . . in my heart." It was an amazing sentence for my granddaughter to have put together all by herself.

"Do you want to ask Jesus to come into your heart, Abigail?"

Smiling, Abigail nodded yes. It seemed as if she had been mulling over this topic for quite some time.

"That's wonderful, sweetheart! What if I say a prayer and you repeat the words after me as best you can, okay?"

"Okay."

Joanna closed her eyes and clasped her daughter's little hand inside her own. Then she prayed: "Dear Jesus . . ."

Abigail didn't hesitate. She was ready to get started. Before Joanna could say anything else, my granddaughter echoed, "Dear Jesus . . ."

Joanna continued, "I believe in you. . . ."

Again, without pausing, Abigail accurately repeated, "I believe in you. . . ."

"Please come into my heart . . . ," said Joanna.

"Please come into my heart . . . ," said Abigail.

"And forgive my sins."

"And forgive my sins," Abigail responded.

Then, speaking together, they said, "Amen."

That was it. Nothing complicated. Just a statement of faith and trust in Christ, plain and simple, as Abigail was able to understand it.

Why do we make things so complicated? When I'm with Abigail, it's a question I often ask myself. Taking life from her vantage point, I find myself laughing more. And worrying less. My senses open up to the sights and sounds I might otherwise miss: doves cooing in the live oak trees by our front porch, raindrops tapping on the roof, a child's cry at the end of the street. My heart is renewed as we relax, play, giggle, sing. Even when I'm in pain. Or tired. Or short on time.

Being with Abigail reminds me to trust God with the burdens that are his business. As I watch her proudly walk down the hall at church with the aid of her braces and a walker, she helps me to understand why my own limitations aren't so important — or even such a hindrance — after all. Her suffering, and she has suffered much, motivates me to look beyond my feelings of helplessness and frustration for heavenly relief.

Spending time with Abigail introduces me to new lessons in faith, and her very life tangibly affirms for me that nothing can happen to anyone without God's permission. Nothing. The moment she was born, the Lord touched my heart with a deep assurance in a way that I had never known before. As I held my newborn granddaughter in my arms for the first time, I felt no fear or doubt concerning God's sovereign design for her life.

Though I had many concerns about the medical procedures she would need, the negative attitudes she would face, the physical challenges she would endure, I knew Abigail was unerringly protected by her Creator. "The Lord watches over you — the Lord is your shade at your right hand; the sun will not harm you by day, nor the moon by night," said a hand-printed notecard I had copied and taped to her crib in the Intensive Care Unit. "The Lord will keep you from all harm — he will watch over your life; the Lord will watch over your coming and going both now and forevermore" (Ps. 121:7–8).

I turn now to the remarkable stories of two women whose courage was fueled by their faith. The first is the Old Testament story of Hagar, told in Genesis. The second is of an early Christian believer, Crispina. Their stories are very different from each other, yet both women learned of God's strengthening presence even as they faced hard times and dark days. They learned the amazing truth: "I can do everything through him who gives me strength" (Phil. 4:13).

Hagar's Story

For years, Abram's wife, Sarai, dreamed of the children she would bear. She pictured their eyes, imagined their voices. Sometimes she even woke herself calling their names, as if they played alongside the tents and crawled after their father. But day after day, the early morning light awakened Sarai to the same bitter reality: Her womb had produced no baby, no son for Abram, no child as God had promised Abram.

Years passed. Sarai grew discouraged and, eventually, despondent. Her monthly cycles, a recurring source of hope and disappointment, grew irregular. Her periods tapered off, then stopped.

Sarai's long-deferred hope sank into frantic desperation. Her daily existence in the desert was difficult enough without having to bear the added shame and sadness of lifelong childlessness. The consuming ache for a child of her own was an unrelenting source of anguish unlike any other emotion Sarai had ever experienced.

Proverbs 30 says there are four things that are never satisfied, and one is "the barren womb." Sarai sensed her dissatisfaction would not end until she held Abram's son, the promised child, in her arms. Still, how could she become pregnant now, at her age?

Sarai had awaited a child from the first day of her marriage. She remembered Abram telling her about God's promise: "Look up at the heavens and count the stars—if indeed you can count them.... So shall your offspring be" (Gen. 15:5).

The words tumbled through Sarai's heart. Finally she could not — would not — continue to maintain the passive stance of a long-suffering wife. Wasn't it her right, even her duty, to act on her husband's behalf?

Sarai was not unfamiliar with the old Assyrian marriage codes, customs, and traditions dealing with the rights of property succession. She knew the local tradition gave infertile wives the right to give their husbands concubines to ensure patrilineage. She and Abram had lived for a while in Egypt, where slaves were used as surrogate mothers. Tablets in Nuzi, a large Mesopotamian city, stated that it was a wife's marital responsibility to give her husband a surrogate if she was unable to provide a male heir.

These secular laws not only allowed Sarai to supply a surrogate for Abram but strictly mandated her to do so. And hadn't the Lord told Abram that an heir would come from *his* body? Had *she* been named as part of the promise?

Sarai quietly considered her options and prepared to move ahead with the business of assuring Abram's family legacy. *Perhaps the Lord has chosen to provide for us in a different way,* Sarai likely thought. *Maybe he has always intended for us to use another means to achieve his purposes. Hagar, my personal maid, could bear the child in my place. Is that it? Lord, is Hagar the woman You intend to be the birth mother of Abram's heir? Why hadn't I realized this before?*

After many years of trusting in God's promise of a child, Sarai stopped waiting.

Walking in the Dark

> *Who among you fears the Lord and obeys the*
> *word of his servant? Let him who walks in the*
> *dark, who has no light, trust in the name of the*
> *Lord and rely on his God.* Isaiah 50:10

Once Sarai had settled her heart on a deliberate course of action, it didn't take long to implement her legally prescribed strategy. It seems there was no discussion.

"The Lord has kept me from having children," she candidly informed Abram, who happened to be her half-brother as well as her husband. "Go, sleep with my maidservant; perhaps I can build a family through her" (Gen. 16:2).

Abram must have been as well-acquainted with the area's traditional marriage norms as his wife was, for without expressing any doubts he agreed to Sarai's plan.

The couple presumably believed their tacit agreement was the proper legal choice. More than likely they also thought it was God's will. What they didn't anticipate, however, was the far-reaching social, emotional, moral, and spiritual damage that would affect everyone involved. Heartbreaking consequences would create widespread conflict, bloodshed, and devastation across the Middle East for generations to come.

When Sarai approached Hagar with the surrogacy plan, we can only imagine what must have gone through the young woman's mind. A slave from Egypt, Hagar was acquainted with the land's laws and local customs. And who knows, Sarai may have offered Hagar a number of attractive incentives to cooperate — better food, improved sleeping accommodations, a new wardrobe.

Hagar must have realized her status would change significantly after sharing Abram's bed: She would be his second wife, a concubine, and possibly the mother of a wealthy heir. In exchange for her fertile womb, the young Egyptian slave was being promised a substantial job promotion.

And so Hagar, full of anxious thoughts and a desperate hope, went to Abram's bed. She bedded her boss's husband. It all went according to Sarai's plan, with one important exception: The act of making a baby with Abram penetrated the heart of Hagar's womanhood. As Hagar opened her body to Abram to receive the gift of life, an intimate bond was created between the two lovers in spite of everyone's best intentions to the contrary.

Is it any wonder, then, that this mutually agreed-upon arrangement ignited in Sarai an intense jealousy? Or that Hagar became proud of her pregnancy and grew to despise her mistress?

Once Hagar conceived, the delicate domestic situation deteriorated. Sarai turned on Abram. "You are responsible for the wrong I am suffering. I put my servant in your arms, and now that she knows she is pregnant, she despises me. May the Lord judge between you and me" (Gen. 16:4–5).

Abram's reply was short: "Your servant is in your hands. Do with her whatever you think best" (Gen. 16:6).

So Sarai demoted Hagar from concubine back to slave. And then she vented her rage on the pregnant handmaiden — the same young woman she had counted on to satisfy her own long-delayed desire for a child.

What a mess. How different things might have been if Sarai had waited in faith upon God's magnificent promise according to the Lord's timing. How might circumstances have changed if Abram and Sarai had kept waiting? We don't know. What we do know is this: The experience of infertility, combined with God's promise of an heir fathered by Abram, proved overwhelming for Sarai. As a result, she believed it was entirely appropriate, perhaps even part of God's plan, to use extreme measures to resolve their excruciating family crisis.

Hagar must have suffered terribly. Within a few months, she had gone from slave to the exalted status of second wife and then was forced back into the role of *shifchah* (the Hebrew word for a woman's personal maidservant). She must have watched in fear as a disturbing change came over her envious, embittered mistress. *What kind of future do I have in this grim household?* When the beatings began, Hagar knew she could stay in Abram's camp no longer. Darkness seemed to engulf her.

Where Are You Going?

> *"I, even I, am he who comforts you."* Isaiah 51:12

Unable to bear her mistress's cruel mistreatment for another minute, Hagar fled into the desert wilderness. Without a clear plan, she simply started running and ran until she could run no longer. Then she walked and walked.

Hours after her departure, Hagar came to her senses and realized the danger she was in. *I forgot to pack any food. I didn't even bring water. What am I going to do? How could I be so stupid? Surely I will die here in the desert, with nothing to eat and no one to tell me where I am going. I'm alone! Lost!*

She collapsed, in tears, next to a spring by the side of the road. She took a long drink from the shimmering pool and sat down to rest. Exhausted, the pregnant traveler slowed her breathing, closed her eyes, and tried to calm herself. Then Hagar heard a Voice, seemingly from out of nowhere.

"Hagar, servant of Sarai, where have you come from, and where are you going?" the Voice asked (Gen. 16: 8).

Hagar had seen no one along the road. Yet here stood a man, looking down at her. Where had he come from? Her mind was a bit fuzzy. Confused. *Who is this man? How does he know my name? Why is he asking me these questions? Why does he care what happens to me?* And yet she felt she could trust him.

She told the stranger, an angel of the Lord, the truth: "I'm running away from my mistress Sarai" (v. 8).

And she thought: *I don't know where I'm going. . . . But what does it matter if I live or die? . . . I have no plan for the future.*

The man spoke again, "Go back to your mistress and submit to her" (v. 9).

Though the words were not what Hagar wanted to hear, she immediately perceived the wisdom in them.

And before the incredulous young woman could respond, the angel gave her a promise: "I will so increase your descendants that they will be too numerous to count" (v. 10).

Hagar suddenly understood who was standing before her — a messenger from Abram's Lord God, maybe even God himself! She tried to stand up, but her limbs felt frozen in place, not from fear but with awe — awe for the unwavering word of truth spoken by the man towering above her, for the tender expression of God's faithful care and concern, for the indescribable majesty of the Lord's holy presence.

"You are now with child and you will have a son," the angel said. "You will name him Ishmael, for the Lord has heard of your misery. He will be a wild donkey of a man; his hand will be against everyone and everyone's hand against him, and he will live in hostility toward all his brothers" (vv. 11–12).

Speaking slowly, almost imperceptibly, Hagar uttered the words that sprang from the very depths of her heart: "You are the God who sees me. I have now seen the One who sees me" (v. 13).

Hagar had seen God and lived, named God and believed, received God and changed. A new strength filled her being as she stood next to the place that would be known from that day forward as Beer Lahai Roi, "the well of the Living One who sees me." Knowing what she must do, Hagar turned back toward Abram's tent and began the long walk home.

Hagar's Return

The Lord will lay bare his holy arm in the sight
of all the nations, and all the ends of the earth
will see the salvation of our God.   Isaiah 52:10

Cast yourself into the arms of God," said Philip Neri, a sixteenth-century Roman evangelist and priest, "and be very sure that if He wants anything of you, He will fit you for the work and give you strength."[3]

Hagar's encounter with God in the desert transformed her life. Though her life previously may have lacked stability and spiritual direction, Hagar now grounded herself in the knowledge that she was no longer without hope, a nonperson. Her suffering had been seen by her Maker. The God who sees had personally promised that she would give birth to a baby boy, to be named Ishmael — "God hears" — a boy whose divinely chosen name would always remind Hagar of her living Lord's watchful care. She would have an inheritance after all.

With great courage Hagar could walk back to Sarai's household because she believed God's words to her: "I will so increase your descendants that they will be too numerous to count." For the rest of her life, Hagar held on to this promise with unrelenting maternal tenacity.

Sarai's *shifchah,* now contrite, awaited the birth of her son. After Ishmael was born, life was easier. Abram, who was eighty-six years old, bonded with his firstborn son and was a good father. Sarai relaxed. The boy became the focal point of their home.

When Ishmael was thirteen, God again spoke to Abram, telling him that he would be the father of many nations. The Lord confirmed his covenant with Abram and gave him a new name — Abraham. As a sign of this binding covenant, the Lord instructed Abraham to be circumcised and to circumcise every male in his household who was eight days old or older. The Lord also told Abraham that Sarai would have a new name: Sarah. "I will bless her and will surely give you a son by her," the Lord promised Abraham. "I will bless her so that she will be the mother of nations; kings of peoples will come from her" (Gen. 17:15–16).

This was too much. Abraham fell facedown and laughed when he heard the news, saying to himself: *Will a son be born to a man a hundred years old? Will Sarah bear a child at the age of ninety?*

Then he thought of Ishmael and appealed to God on behalf of his adolescent son: "If only Ishmael might live under your blessing!" (Gen. 17:18). Prompted by his father-love, Abraham could not restrain himself from telling God that he genuinely desired Ishmael's highest good. It was as if the old man had not even heard God say that Sarah would

have a son who would be Abraham's true heir, the child of
the promise.

The Lord did not rebuke Ishmael's father, but patiently
responded: "Yes, but your wife Sarah will bear you a son,
and you will call him Isaac. I will establish my covenant with
him as an everlasting covenant for his descendants after him.
And as for Ishmael, I have heard you: I will surely bless him;
I will make him fruitful and will greatly increase his num-
bers. He will be the father of twelve rulers and I will make
him into a great nation" (Gen. 17:19–20).

Then, as if Abraham still needed to hear the words one
more time, God repeated: "But my covenant I will establish
with Isaac, whom Sarah will bear to you by this time next
year" (Gen. 17:21).

Later that day, Abraham circumcised every male in his
household, including thirteen-year-old Ishmael — who
became the first bar mitzvah! Hagar's return had not only
saved her life but spared the life of her son and given him
inheritance rights in Abraham's household. Ishmael and his
heirs would receive a measure of God's blessing due to their
close ties with Abraham. Though he would not be the full
heir of the promise, Abraham's firstborn son would receive
God's blessing of fruitfulness — twelve sons! — and the estab-
lishment of a great nation through Ishmael's prolific progeny.

Within a year, Sarah gave birth to the promised son,
Isaac. Ishmael continued to enjoy Abraham's daily companionship. Hagar faithfully served her mistress and her son.
But life changed again when Isaac was weaned, and Ishmael
was Abraham's preferred son no longer.

The Wilderness of Paran

> *Seek the Lord while he may be found;*
> *call on him while he is near.* Isaiah 55:6

At Isaac's weaning feast, a grand event that officially announced the boy's biological separation from his mother and commemorated his emerging manhood, Sarah noticed a disturbing sign of sibling rivalry. Ishmael laughed at Isaac. Now that Isaac was no longer a little child nursing at his mother's breast, he was going to need much more of Abraham's personal tutoring and attention.

As always, Sarah was straightforward with her husband. "Get rid of that slave woman and her son, for that slave woman's son will never share in the inheritance of my son Isaac" (Gen. 21:10).

The harsh words pierced Abraham's heart. He dearly loved Ishmael. The thought of his firstborn boy, now a fine young man, departing from his household deeply distressed him. Yet Sarah's words conveyed a truth — that God's plan for Israel would be revealed through Isaac, not Ishmael.

Scripture says the Lord himself told Abraham: "Do not be upset over the boy and your servant wife. Do just as Sarah says, for Isaac is the son through whom your descendants will be counted. But I will make a nation of the descendants of Hagar's son because he is also your son" (Gen. 21:12–13 NLB).

God's words must have given Abraham precisely the strength he needed to perform the awful task: He awoke first thing the next morning, prepared some provisions, strapped a skin of water on Hagar's shoulders, and sent his second wife with their first son into the scorching wilderness.

Abraham's farewell token of food and water didn't last long. Disoriented by grief and broken in spirit, Hagar and Ishmael wandered aimlessly across the desert of Beersheba for days as their rations dwindled. They ate and drank lightly, yet the supply was going, going, and finally gone. When Hagar went to pour out a handful of water for her son and noticed the skin was empty, she fully comprehended the scope of their desperate situation.

Hagar looked at Ishmael. He was nearly an adult, yes, but she had always been able to see the playful young child dwelling inside his manly skin — the mischievous glint in his eyes, his countless curious looks, his immense physical energy. But not now. Tears welled up in her eyes as she saw death begin to erase the light that had always shone through his countenance.

Hagar placed Ishmael under a small bush, which provided a little shade. She stood beside him for a moment. The pace of his breathing had changed. Her son was dying and there was nothing she could do to save his life.

Hagar walked a bowshot away from her son and began to cry.

"I cannot watch the boy die," Hagar wailed (Gen. 21:16). *Please God. Please. Please. Please.*

Though Hagar did not hear him, Ishmael — whose name, remember, meant "God hears" — was crying, too.

And the Lord was listening.

"What is the matter, Hagar?" Ah, it was the Voice, a sound she had never forgotten and often remembered. A Voice unlike any other — fiercely protective, solid as stone, refreshing as the summer rain that falls on desert flowers in the late afternoon. So soothing and startling. So real. "Do not be afraid; God has heard the boy crying as he lies there.

Lift the boy up and take him by the hand, for I will make him into a great nation" (Gen. 21:17–18).

As Hagar stood up, "God opened her eyes" (v. 19). There, right before her, was a well of water. No mirage. The real thing. She felt the water run through her fingers. It washed away days' worth of dust. She filled the skin and carried the water of life to her son.

In the parched days and long dry years that followed, Hagar surely found the faith and courage to carry out her daily tasks of desert survival as a single mother by drawing near to the living God who had heard her cries for help, seen her need for sustenance, and opened her eyes to discover the Lord's miraculous last-minute, lifesaving provision. With God's help, Hagar made her home with Ishmael in the Desert of Paran, where the Lord remained with the boy as he grew up and became an archer, just as the angel had prophesied.

Crispina of Thagora's Story

❧

*L*iving by faith — trusting in God — does not mean we believe that God, our genie in heaven, will shoo away every bad guy who harasses us. Our trust is in God's presence and providence, his love and ultimate good purpose. Throughout history, even in our generation, men and women have courageously laid down their very lives as their ultimate act of trust in God.

The word "martyr," based on the Greek term *martus*, means "witness." The costly calling of martyrdom is the most courageous form of taking a stand in faith for the sake of our Savior. "No one is a martyr for a conclusion; no one is a martyr for an opinion; it is faith that makes martyrs," observed John Henry Newman, the nineteenth-century Anglican leader of the Oxford movement.[4]

During the first three centuries of our faith, martyrdom was not uncommon among Christians who openly confessed their belief in Jesus. Countless ancient graves in Italy, Greece, Africa, and Asia Minor contain the remains of martyrs who refused to worship Rome's pagan gods. Torture, imprisonment, and death awaited many who professed faith in Jesus Christ. No distinction was accorded to a person's age, social rank, profession, age, or gender. Babies, noblewomen, soldiers, and great-grandmothers alike perished in the terrible persecutions.

"Christianity is warfare, and Christians spiritual soldiers," Robert Southwell perceptively noted in the sixteenth century. "In its beginning, our faith was planted in the poverty, infamy, persecution and death of Christ; in its progress, it was watered by the blood of God's saints; and it cannot come to full growth unless it be fostered with the showers of the martyrs' blood."[5] Though it is difficult to consider the trials and tribulations of Christians persecuted for their faith, my faith — and I trust yours — is deepened by reading stories of Christian martyrs, such as Crispina, because their willingness to face death for the sake of Christ encourages me to draw closer to heaven's unchanging reality.

Crispina lived under the rule of Roman Emperor Diocletian (A.D. 284–305), who was responsible for the last persecution of Christians in the Roman Empire, commonly called the Era of the Martyrs. We know her story from a reliable firsthand account written by a friend who was present at her trial and execution; it now belongs to a larger body of writings known as the *Acta* (Acts of the Martyrs).[6]

Let's set the stage: Diocletian's reign of terror may have been fed by the increased visibility and affluence of an increasing number of Christians and the persistent influence of Diocletian's adopted son Galerius, whose hatred for Christians was goaded by his mother's extreme pagan bigotry. Diocletian's persecution dramatically accelerated on February 23, 303, as he, his wife, and Galerius celebrated Terminalia — their scheme to terminate Christianity.

The horrors began with a raid upon a church in Nicodemia, when scores of officers and governmental officials broke in and seized every sacred book in the building — Scriptures that had painstakingly been printed by hand. Diocletian and Galerius personally supervised a book bonfire and then ordered the church to be leveled to the ground.

From that day on, the emperor's persecution plan escalated. He ordered the destruction of all Christian churches, sacred writings, and books, and he declared all Christians "outlaws," subject to arrest and execution. Across the Roman Empire, followers of Christ were seized, tortured, massacred — beheaded, drowned, hanged, torn apart by wild beasts, and buried alive. An entire city in Phrygia — buildings and inhabitants — was incinerated, Diocletian believing that everyone who lived there was a Christian convert.

Many lives were spared when several provincial governors eventually complained about the rampant use of racks, scourges, spears, crosses, poison, and famine to kill Christians. Even so, Diocletian and Galerius continued their campaign of torture: cutting off ears, slitting noses, gouging out right eyes, permanently maiming limbs, branding flesh.

Galerius was personally responsible for the torture and execution of many Christian women, including Crispina. Highly educated, from a prominent noble family in Thagora, in northern Africa, Crispina was married and the mother of several children. Her serene and courageous testimony, dignified self-defense, and calm assurance under extreme pressure still stand as a vibrant witness to us today.

The Interrogation at Tebessa

In my distress, I called to the Lord; I cried to God for help.
From his temple he heard my voice; my cry came before
him, into his ears. Psalm 18:6

*D*ecember 5, 304. Crispina stood outside the council chamber of Judge Annius Anullinus, in the North African colony of Tebessa, awaiting, awaiting her earthly fate.[7]
The clerk of the court presented the next case to Anullinus: "Crispina of Thagora has defied the laws of our

lords the emperors. She can be heard if you give the order."

"Bring her in," the judge said.

The matronly woman walked in and stood respectfully before the judge, who spoke directly to her, "Do you know the text of the emperor's religious edict?"

"No, sir. What does the order say?"

The judge read the edict aloud: "All citizens are required to offer sacrifice to all our gods for the welfare of the emperors according to the law issued by the *Augusti* Diocletian and Maximian and our most noble Caesars, Constantius and Maximus."

Crispina replied quickly and honestly: "I have never sacrificed and never will, save to the one true God and to our Savior Jesus Christ, his Son, who was born, suffered, and died."

Anullinus persisted. "Renounce your superstitious beliefs. Bow your head and worship Rome's gods."

No. Crispina was going to hold her ground. "Every day I worship and call upon my almighty God. I know no other gods but him."

Anullinus kept pushing the issue. "You are stubborn, scornful, and out of your mind. And you will soon learn the cost of your insolence."

Still no. *I will not renounce my faith. I will not be pressured.* "Whatever happens, I will readily suffer it in the name of the faith I hold firm."

The judge seemed incredulous. *Does this woman know what she is doing? This is no uneducated back-country woman.* He prodded her again: "Are you so stupid — to obstinately cling to the crazy superstition rather than worship our most holy deities?"

He's not getting this, is he? God, help me remain steadfast. Help me. "I worship every single day—the true and living God. He alone is my Lord. Besides him, I know no other."

It seemed as though Anullinus did not want to see this woman die. "I repeat the sacred edict: Obey the emperor's command."

One more time. "I will obey only the command given by my Lord Jesus Christ."

The warning now came with a horrifying image: "I will have your head cut off if you do not submit to the edicts of the emperors. You are legally obligated to obey them. You must yield to their authority. What's more, all of Africa has offered these sacrifices, as you probably realize."

Crispina's hand went to her neck, but she remained calm. "Nothing you say or do will ever make me sacrifice to demons. I sacrifice to the Lord who made heaven and earth, the sea, and all that is in them."

More Pressure

> *They confronted me in the day of my disaster, but the Lord was my support.* Psalm 18:18

Anullinus continued his inquisition: "So—our deities are not acceptable to you! And yet you are obligated to serve these gods you disdain if you want to keep living and practice any worship at all!"

Crispina inserted a reproof—"Any religion that inflicts torture on those who do not adhere to it is worthless"—which Anullinus shrugged off: "No matter."

But he tried again to dissuade her: "Whatever your religion, all we are asking is for you to bow your head when you are in the sacred temples and give incense offerings to Rome's gods."

Crispina would not be worn down. "From the time I was born until now, I have never done this. I have always been a stranger to your religious rites and will remain so for as long as I live."

"But you must do so now if you hope to escape the severity of the law's sanctions."

With a steady, calm voice, Crispina replied: "Your threats do not frighten me; they are nothing. But if I deliberately commit a sacrilege, my God who is in heaven will abandon me and I will not be found in him on the last day."

"Someone who submits to the sacred edicts is not committing sacrilege!" Anullinus retorted.

Crispina's voice rose a bit as she said: "May these gods who did not make heaven and earth perish altogether! I sacrifice to the eternal living God who abides forever and ever. He is the true God who is to be feared — the Maker of the sea, the green fields, the desert sand. What can I possibly fear from those who are only the creatures of his hand?"

The judge said, "Revere the Roman religion, like our lords, the undefeated Caesars, and all the rest of us." Was it an angry command or was he begging her to spare him from having to hand down the fateful sentence?

"I have told you: I am prepared to endure any tortures you may inflict," Crispina replied, "but I will never defile my soul with stone idols made by men's hands."

"Your words are blasphemy. Woman, you are not aiding your cause," Anullinus explained with great clarity. "If you so disdain and despise the worship of our sacred deities, I will cut off your head."

The End of Life, the Beginning of Glory

*For I have kept the ways of the Lord; I have not done evil
by turning from my God.* Psalm 18:21

Anullinus looked at the court clerk and commanded,
"Shame this woman: Have her hair cut and her head
shaved with a razor until she is bald. First, let her face feel
this outrage!"

At this point Crispina responded: "Let your gods speak
now, and I will believe. I would not even be here in your tri-
bunal if I weren't seriously seeking my salvation."

"Don't you want to live a long time?" Anullinus retorted.
"Or would you actually prefer to die in torment, like so
many of your companions?"

"If I wished to perish and surrender my soul to the pain
of eternal fire, yes — I would put my faith in your demons."

Anullinus repeated his ultimate threat: "I will cut off
your head if you persist in your refusal to venerate our
sacred gods."

Crispina seemed strengthened in her resolve, newly
invigorated. "I should gladly give thanks to God if I obtained
such an end, and will wholeheartedly accept having my head
cut off for my Lord. For I absolutely refuse to sacrifice to
these illusory deaf-and-dumb statues."

"So you are determined to maintain your crazy resolu-
tion?" Anullinus said, looking carefully at the woman before
him.

Without wavering, Crispina paid homage to the God
who had seen and heard Hagar, the God who was seeing and
hearing Crispina's own faithful and courageous witness: "My
God who is and who remains eternal commanded my birth;

he brought me salvation and brought me through the living waters of baptism: He is with me, at my side, supporting and helping me, strengthening his handmaid in all her trials and difficulties. Thanks to the Lord, I shall not commit sacrilege."

Realizing that his questioning had been completely ineffectual, Anullinus requested that the minutes of the trial be read. That done, he announced the dreadful sentence which had been written on a tablet: "Seeing that Crispina has persisted in her infamous superstition and refuses to sacrifice to our gods in accordance with the heavenly decrees of the sacred Augustan law, I ordain that she be executed with the sword."

Before sundown that very day, Crispina met her Maker. Her last words were: "I bless my God who has so deigned to free me from your hands. Thanks be to God!" After making the sign of the cross on her forehead and laying her head on the block, Crispina lost her life. Walking through the dark valley of death, she feared no evil and was ushered into the presence of the Light of this world and the world to come.

Part of Crispina's trial testimony has been translated into a prayer form, expressing her unyielding faith, showing her dependence on God — the source of her strength and courage. May we make this prayer our own:

O God, who was and is,
* you willed that I should be born.*
You brought me to salvation
* through the waters of baptism.*
Be with me now and strengthen my soul
* that I will not weaken.*
Praise to God who has looked upon me
* and delivered me from my enemies.*[8]

— Crispina of Thagora

Abide with me! Fast falls the eventide.
The darkness deepens; Lord, with me abide!
When other helpers fail and comforts flee,
Help of the helpless, O abide with me!

Swift to its close ebbs out life's little day.
Earth's joys grow dim; its glories pass away.
Change and decay in all around I see;
O Thou who changest not, abide with me!

I need Thy presence every passing hour.
What but Thy grace can foil the tempter's power?
Who, like Thyself, my guide and stay can be?
Through cloud and sunshine, O abide with me!

I fear no foe, with Thee at hand to bless;
Ills have no weight, and tears no bitterness.
Where is death's sting? Where, grave, thy victory?
I triumph still if Thou abide with me!

Hold Thou Thy cross before my closing eyes;
Shine through the gloom, and point me to the skies.
Heaven's morning breaks, and earth's vain shadows flee!
In life, in death, O Lord, abide with me!

— Henry F. Lyte (1793–1847)

Conclusion

Crispina boldly said that she would "wholeheartedly accept" martyrdom for her Lord. What an incredible statement: Commitment to Jesus Christ requires wholehearted trust. But our ability to depend on the Lord requires supernatural strength — the kind of radical reliance on God that can be produced in us only by the Holy Spirit working within our lives. Whether we see faith as a gift or as a fruit, it does not originate with us — though we can choose to accept it or choose to allow it to grow.

Moment by moment, we can choose to trust the Lord to lead us, strengthen us, and sustain us. For Hagar, faith meant life and posterity. For Crispina, faith meant a martyr's death.

We, like them, can discover that our willingness to trust God in the midst of life's most difficult circumstances becomes a form of holy protection no matter how dark our surroundings may appear. Hebrews chapter 11 gives a long list of Old Testament heroes of faith. The writer challenges you and me: "Let us fix our eyes on Jesus, the author and perfecter of our faith, who for the joy set before him endured the cross, scorning its shame, and sat down at the right hand of the throne of God. Consider him who endured such opposition from sinful men, so that you will not grow weary and lose heart" (Heb. 12:2–3). Fix your eyes on the One who perfects your faith — so you will have courage.

This passage — and many others — indicate that Jesus himself endured hardship. Sometimes we ache to know the "why?" behind our suffering or someone else's suffering. The gifted preacher Charles Spurgeon understood that trials, troubles, and tribulations are part of every person's experience. When a series of tragic disasters, including a railroad accident, struck Great Britain early in September 1861, Spurgeon delivered a sermon in London about God's unfathomable providence. In this sermon, titled "Accidents, Not Punishments," he said:

> If a calamity were always the result of some sin, providence would be as simple as that twice two made four. It would be one of the first lessons that a child might learn. But Scripture teaches us that providence is a great depth in which the human intellect may swim and dive, but it can find neither a bottom nor a shore. If you and I pretend that we can find out the reasons of providence and twist the dispensations of God over our fingers, we only prove our folly, but we do not prove that we have begun to understand the ways of God. . . .
>
> Do you not know that the great transactions of providence began six thousand years ago? You have only stepped into this world for thirty or forty years and have seen only one actor on the stage, and you say you understand it. You have only begun to know. Only God knows the end from the beginning; only He understands what are the great results, what is the great reason for which the world was made and for which He permits both good and evil to occur. Think not that you know the ways of God. It is to degrade providence and to bring God down to the level of men when you pretend you can understand those calamities and find out the secret designs of wisdom.

But next, do you not perceive that such an idea as this would encourage Pharisaism? The people who were crushed to death or scalded or destroyed under the wheels of railway trains were worse sinners than we are? . . . I have never read in the Scriptures, "We know that we have passed from death unto life because we have traveled from London to Bristol safely twice a day."[9]

As the Holy Spirit leads us into a deepening awareness of Jesus' lordship over all of life's experiences — no matter how confusing, difficult, or painful our circumstances may become — our thoughts and feelings find a reliable shelter under the covering of Christ's unfailing love and protective authority.

"The sovereignty of God is the one impregnable rock to which the suffering human heart must cling. The circumstances surrounding our lives are no accident: they may be the work of evil, but evil is held firmly within the mighty hand of our sovereign God," clarifies Margaret Carlson in her book *Grace Grows Best in Winter.* She continues: "All evil is subject to Him, and evil cannot touch His children unless He permits it. God is the Lord of human history and of the personal history of every member of his redeemed family."[10]

No human being can fully understand the full range of life's experiences this side of eternity, but the King of heaven already understands what we're going through — and why. Though we can't see God, our faith gives us confidence that Hagar's "God who sees and hears" is the *God who sees and hears us* and is continually working for our good in all of life's circumstances, no matter how things may appear to happen.

"I am the light of the world," said Jesus. "Whoever follows me will never walk in darkness, but will have the light of life" (John 8:12). When we don't know the "why" behind what we're going through, we can trust the Lord to light the way ahead. Even in the darkness.

Points for Reflection

1. These stories encourage me to trust Christ wholeheartedly when I face . . .
2. Knowing that God's purposes for my life cannot be thwarted helps me to . . .
3. Hagar's response to hearing God's voice caused me to think about . . .
4. I find it especially difficult to trust God when . . .
5. When I consider Crispina's testimony in the face of her persecutors, I am amazed by . . .
6. For me, trusting God in and through the darkness means . . .

Prayer: Lord, *in You there is no darkness at all. Help me to trust You with all my heart. How I need You to keep reminding me of what is most important — about why I am here, and where I am going, and who is in control. Thank you for the immense security of Your steadfast love, for the powerful protection of Your living Word, for the unshakable truth of Your everlasting promises. Guide my path as I walk with You today and always, in Jesus' name, I pray. Amen.*

*The Lord is faithful to all his promises
and loving toward all he has made.
The Lord upholds all those who fall
and lifts up all who are bowed down.
The eyes of all look to you,
and you give them their food at the proper time.
You open your hand
and satisfy the desires of every living thing.*

*The Lord is righteous in all his ways
and loving toward all he has made.
The Lord is near to all who call on him,
to all who call on him in truth.
He fulfills the desires of those who fear him;
he hears their cry and saves them.*

— Psalm 145:13–19

Acceptance says, True, this is my situation at the moment. I'll look unblinking at the reality of it. But I'll also open my hands to accept willingly whatever a loving Father sends.[11]

— Catherine Marshall, 1914–1983

Does the road wind up hill all the way?
  Yes, to the very end.
Will the day's journey take the whole long day?
  From morn to night, my friend.

But is there for the night a resting place?
  A roof for when the slow dark hours begin.
May not the darkness hide it from my face?
  You cannot miss that inn.

Shall I meet other wayfarers at night?
  Those who have gone before.
Then must I knock, or call when just in sight?
  They will not keep you at that door.

Shall I find comfort, travel sore and weak?
  Of labour you shall find the sum.
Will there be beds for me and all who seek?
  Yea, beds for all who come.[12]

  — Christina Rossetti (1830–1894), "Uphill"

Chapter Two

❦

For Love

The knowledge of God is very far from the love of Him.[1]

— Blaise Pascal (1623–1662)

We love because he first loved us" (1 John 4:19).
Have you often found yourself feeling frustrated, exasperated, or amazed by love? Do you sometimes try to grasp the magnificent, satisfying fullness of love only to find yourself face to face with its apparent limits and limitations?

How easy it is to become discouraged in our continuing quest to give and receive love. In those sublime moments when the Lord blesses us with his compassion, patience, mercy, and grace, we again learn the lesson: Love does not originate in us, but in God. Like it or not, we can love only when God is the source, the substance, and the completion of our love.

Still, we live in a world where it seems perfectly natural to forget whom love really comes from, a world where love and loss intermingle in confusing patterns. Most of us discover early in life this can be quite difficult to sort out, let alone accept or understand.

In the midst of our tears and sorrow, loneliness and rejection, it isn't unusual to feel ourselves standing at a distance from the love our heavenly Father freely offers. Our sadness, frustration, and anger over life's circumstances may cause us to close up our hearts rather than reach out to more fully embrace Christ's steady comfort, mercy, and compassion in the midst of our less-than-perfect, real-life circumstances.

For my friend Diane, an overbooked schedule suddenly screeched to a halt with a serious case of burn-out. Only then did she stop and spend some serious time in the Word.

There she learned that "perhaps the most amazing thing about the Lord's unwavering care for me is that he continues to comfort and strengthen me even when I get overloaded or bogged down under the weighty burdens of my own making. With unmistakable clarity his Word over and over again sends its incredible message: *You are loved*.

"I think I'm going to spend the rest of my life learning the meaning of that incredible phrase, getting it down into the innermost center of my being," she continues. "It isn't an easy truth to grow into, even in the areas of my heart where I'm most hungry for it, where I need to receive love's healing the most. Still, the Spirit's main job is to teach me this lesson, moment by moment, until I eventually awaken in glory and reach the end of my rambling once and for all."

We love because he first loved us. Not because we can live free from troubles, trials, and temptations if we love. Not because of what God will do for us if we love him or what others will (maybe) do for us if we love them. Not even because love is right. Or good. Or best.

"Some may question if God deserves our love or if they might have something to gain by loving him. The answer to both questions is yes, but I find no other worthy reason for loving him except himself," Bernard of Clairvaux, a twelfth-century monk, observed. "God is clearly deserving of our love especially if we consider who he is that loves us, who we are that he loves, and how much he loves us."[2]

We love because he first loved us — and in loving God, we find our greatest delight, our highest joy, our deepest peace, our brightest vision, our strongest shelter. As we live in his love, we welcome the Lord's unchanging, attentive presence and feel at home dwelling in his courts of praise, on good days and bad. Revived and refreshed through prayer and worship, we are renewed with the Spirit's power, no matter what we're going through. Or how much we've failed to live up to our own and others' expectations.

"I trust in your unfailing love," wrote David, who himself was well acquainted with personal failure, vicious persecution, spiritual brokenness, and marital tragedy (Ps. 13:5). Like God's beloved psalmist, we also gain some understanding of what it means to love ourselves and others for Christ's sake — for his uses and purposes, plans and intentions, instead of just our own — as we cling to the Lord's steadfast love through the changing seasons of our lives.

It's guaranteed: Life will reliably teach us that love is much more than a feeling, a duty, an act of giving, a moment of forgiveness, a romantic adventure, or a resolute decision to seek someone else's highest good. And it's when our thirst for God grows through unplanned encounters with life's rough terrain and rugged desert places we can best realize: "All my fountains are in you" (Ps. 87:7).

Like the unnamed woman living in obscurity in the following story, we discover that if we're willing to keep seeking our Savior, we eventually learn that the Lord's unfailing love for us is far deeper and truer and braver than we ever dreamed it could be — a truth we also see clearly reflected in the story of a fifteenth-century saint named Catherine of Genoa.

The Samaritan Woman's Story

✤

He wasn't supposed to be there.

She could tell by the way he was dressed, the unshaven beard, his Galilean garments. He was Jewish. Yet here he was, sitting alone beside Jacob's well just outside Sychar, a Samaritan city.

It didn't make any sense. Who was he waiting for? Why had he stopped *here* of all places?

His intensely focused demeanor made her wonder if he might be a rabbi — a teacher of the Torah, an interpreter of the Law. Given his simple, slightly ragged appearance, she suspected that the dust-covered young man, like her, was poor.

It was midday. The sun was high in the sky. Had the weary rabbi become so disoriented by the heat that he had lost his way?

Jewish people traveling between Galilee in the north and Judea in the south usually took great pains to cross the Jordan River to avoid going through Samaria. The conflict between the Jews and Samaritans had existed for two centuries, ever since the Assyrians had banished Abraham's descendants from the area and repopulated the country with commoners from the north. The Jews especially detested these imported settlers. Though the Samaritans did have weak familial ties to the Hebrew tribes, they were considered unclean, an idol-worshiping people who arrogantly presumed to share a spiritual inheritance with God's chosen ones.

He was Jewish. She was a Samaritan. Maybe just as significant in terms of social alienation, he was a man, she was a woman. In Jewish culture of New Testament times, the gender gap was wide. A man did not talk to a woman without her husband present.

That background sets the stage for one of the most significant conversations recorded in the gospel of John, between Jesus and "the Samaritan woman."

No More Secrets

> *The Spirit of the Sovereign Lord is upon me, because the Lord has anointed me to preach good news to the poor. He has sent me to bind up the brokenhearted, to proclaim freedom for the captives and release from darkness for the prisoners.* Isaiah 61:1

The Samaritan woman approached the well to get her day's supply of water. As she drew near, she heard the man say, with no hint of hesitation in his voice, "Will you give me a drink?" (John 4:7).

She didn't think she had correctly heard the question. She couldn't understand why this man desired her hospitality. She was a Samaritan, a woman, and what's more — and he would have known this — any *respectable* woman drew water early in the morning, not at noontime.

She'd come to the well in the middle of the day because she knew no one else would be there. Years of unkindness and social discrimination had convinced her she was better off avoiding contact with her neighbors. She had grown accustomed to drawing and carrying the water alone, in silence. But now someone — a Jewish man! — had spoken to her. Why?

She had nothing to lose. She took a chance and matter-of-factly challenged the man's request. "You are a Jew and I am a Samaritan woman," she explained, pointing out the obvious. "How can you ask me for a drink?" (John 4:9).

She watched him carefully. With the experienced eyes of someone who was used to evaluating hypocrisy and human weakness, she marked the moment when the stranger's gaze fastened on hers.

It was odd, the way he looked at her, the way he sat there so quietly, as if he had all the time in the world and didn't care what anyone might think about a Jewish man and a Samaritan woman casually conversing at Jacob's well in the middle of the day.

The man seemed to know her, yet there was no hint of impropriety in his gaze. If she had been asked at that moment to describe what she saw in his countenance, she probably would have said: Sweetness. And light.

"If you knew the gift of God and who it is who asks you for a drink," the man gently informed her, "you would have asked him and he would have given you living water" (John 4:10).

Again, she couldn't tell whether she had heard correctly. Was this one of those famous Hebrew riddles she had heard about? What was he trying to say? Was he offering to get water from the well for her? If so, how would he, without any container?

"Sir," she said, "you have nothing to draw the water with and the well is deep. Where can you get this living water? Are you greater than our father Jacob, who gave us the well and drank from it himself, as did also his sons and his flocks and herds?" (John 4:11–12).

She would always remember the sound of his reply as it sprang from a source deeper than the well, truer than the sunrise, larger than the heavens: "Everyone who drinks this water will be thirsty again, but whoever drinks the water I give him will never thirst. Indeed, the water I give him will become in him a spring of water welling up to eternal life" (John 4:13–14).

What was he saying? What did he mean? What kind of man would make this astonishing claim? What kind of man would promise . . . ?

"Sir," she said boldly, with more than a little hopeful anticipation, "give me this water so that I won't get thirsty and have to keep coming here to draw water" (John 4:15).

Suddenly he changed the subject: "Go, call your husband and come back" (John 4:16).

Go, call your husband and come back, she repeated to herself. What can I say? He will never want to give me God's gift once he knows who I am. What I've done. Where I've been. Whom I've slept with.

Why would he?

Still, she found she had absolutely no desire to answer him with anything less than complete honesty. So she looked at the stranger, this man she thought might be a rabbi, and told him the truth. "I have no husband."

That's when he said one of the most surprising things of all: "You are right when you say you have no husband."

She felt her cheeks grow warm. Her hands turn cold. Her stomach clench. Her chest tighten.

How did he know?

Yet there was no turning away from this humble, enigmatic man who spoke to her so plainly and directly, with such great compassion and clear conviction. She stood there and listened in spite of her terrible discomfort.

His voice was calm and even as he explained, "The fact is, you have had five husbands, and the man you now have

is not your husband. What you have just said is quite true"
(John 4:18).

Looking for Love

> *... to proclaim the year of the Lord's favor and the day of*
> *vengeance of our God, to comfort all who mourn, and*
> *provide for those who grieve in Zion — to bestow on them*
> *a crown of beauty instead of ashes, the oil of joy instead*
> *of mourning, and a garment of praise instead of a*
> *spirit of despair.* Isaiah 61:2–3

The man was right. She had been married five times.
She had also experienced the pain and anguish of
divorce five times as each of her husbands chose to reject
her — in a continuing chain of humiliating marital disgrace.

She hadn't been unfaithful to any of them. (The city's
religious leaders would have stoned her for that.) After her
first marriage fell apart, it wasn't long before her next husband delivered her a note of divorce. Then the next. For the
law the Samaritans had adopted from the Pentateuch said:

If a man marries a woman who becomes displeasing
to him because he finds something indecent about her,
and he writes her a certificate of divorce, gives it to her
and sends her from his house, and if after she leaves
his house she becomes the wife of another man, and
her second husband dislikes her and writes her a certificate of divorce, gives it to her and sends her from
his house, or if he dies, then her first husband, who
divorced her, is not allowed to marry her again after
she has been defiled. (Deuteronomy 24:1–4)

No woman was allowed to divorce her husband, yet a man could legally and easily cast off his wife for a wide variety of reasons. How could she have known that the definition of *indecent* could be legally construed to mean almost anything in those days? That she could be rejected not once but five times by husbands who did not find her pleasing enough. Beautiful enough. Good enough.

Why had she kept trying for so long, through so many marriages and divorces, to find a man who would return her love? Why had she continued to believe that just because a man wanted to marry her — as five of them had, proving that she was a desirable mate, at least initially — he would continue to care for her for the rest of her life?

Most women would have given up the search for love long ago. But she was a dreamer, an idealist. A fool.

Finally, the multiple rejections encased her heart inside a brittle emotional coldness, like the frost that covers the desert mountains in late winter. She vowed never to marry again. She avoided contact with people. She grew accustomed to her aloneness. She convinced herself that the dense silence of her isolation was preferable to the unwelcome intrusions of her tactless neighbors.

Forget them, she often would say to herself. *It doesn't matter what they think. Ever since I stopped listening to the latest gossip and started ignoring those self-righteous hypocrites, I've discovered how little I need from them.*

To a certain extent, the long hours of isolated reflection had been beneficial, provoking her to think about a number of theological concepts she hadn't previously considered, causing her to seek honest answers to the intriguing spiritual questions she had only recently started to learn about and contemplate.

She sensed that the appearance of this man, this unconventional meeting with a Jew who knew so much about her, wasn't a mere accident.

Spirit and Truth

> *Instead of their shame, my people will receive a double portion, and instead of disgrace, they will rejoice in their inheritance; and so they will inherit a double portion in their land, and everlasting joy will be theirs.* Isaiah 61:7

In an instant, it became clear to her that she no longer needed to pretend, that she had nothing to lose by diving deeper into the conversation she had been wanting to have for so long while not once believing it would ever really happen.

"Sir," she began, "I can see that you are a prophet. Our fathers worshiped on this mountain, but you Jews claim that the place where we must worship is in Jerusalem" (John 4:19–20).

This wasn't a statement that most women would make to a man. This wasn't a discussion that most Samaritans would have with a Jew. Yet the young man was not offended.

"Believe me, the time is coming when it will no longer matter whether you worship the Father here or in Jerusalem," he said. "You Samaritans know so little about the one you worship, while we Jews know all about him, for salvation comes through the Jews. But the time is coming and is already here when true worshipers will worship the Father in spirit and truth. The Father is looking for anyone who will worship him that way. For God is Spirit, so those who worship him must worship in spirit and in truth" (John 4:21–24 NLB).

What kind of Jewish religious teacher dared to speak of such things to a Samaritan, let alone a woman? It was as if he already knew what she had been secretly studying and thinking about. She wasn't interested in Taheb, the Samaritans' expected spiritual deliverer — she was seeking the Lord.

"I know that Messiah" (called Christ) "is coming," she told him confidently. "When he comes, he will explain everything to us" (John 4:25).

In that still, small moment just before he answered her, she could feel the sun's warmth on her back and could hear the sound of the wind as it rushed through the olive trees. She smoothed the folds of her apron, set her water jar down beside the well, and lifted her eyes to meet his.

"I am the Messiah!" (John 4:26 NLB).

I am the Messiah.

Later, as she pictured his face and played back the words in her mind, she realized: *I have never felt as alive as I did at that moment. It was as if time and space slipped away and reality itself became more real, less distant, closer than the air in my lungs, nearer than the pulse of my heartbeat. For an instant, neither the past nor the future seemed to matter. I was aware of only one thing — his absolute love.*

Soon the disciples, who had gone off to find some lunch, returned to Jesus at the well. When they arrived, the Samaritan woman left her water jar behind and ran toward the town, where she immediately told others about what she had heard. No longer was she afraid of their rejection.

"Come, see a man who told me everything I ever did," the exhilarated messenger announced, unable to contain her joy and amazement any longer. "Could this be the Christ?" (John 4:29). Assured of Jesus' love, she found the courage to openly share the incredible story of what had just happened at Jacob's well. She had to share her good news with others, regardless of what they might think. Transformed by God's love, she became one of the first evangelists to proclaim the Gospel.

Upon hearing her testimony, many of the Samaritans in Sychar believed in Christ. The townspeople urged Jesus to stay with them a little longer. He remained with them for two days and "because of his words many more became believers" (John 4:41). And after the Messiah left, the people said to her, "We no longer believe just because of what you said; now we have heard for ourselves, and we know that this man really is the Savior of the world" (John 4:42).

Catherine of Genoa's Story

❧

The courageous life of Catherine Fieschi Adorno was full of wild, colorful contrasts: a worldly aristocrat's daughter who became famous for her "otherworldliness" following her dramatic conversion experience; a child bride locked into a loveless marriage who surrendered her broken heart to God and later witnessed her husband's remarkable encounter with the Lord's redemptive grace; a nurse and hospital administrator who gave forty years of selfless service to the sick and dying poor of her hometown even as she cultivated a largely hidden life of contemplative prayer.

Catherine was born in the autumn of 1447, the youngest of five children. Her family, the Fieschis, was considered the greatest of the old patrician Guelph families of Genoa in Italy. By the mid-fifteenth century, Catherine's family was at the peak of its power, wealth, and influence. Her ancestral family included two popes as well as numerous cardinals, lords, and nobles. Her father was the Viceroy of Naples.

Catherine grew up alongside her three boisterous older brothers and her devout sister, Limbania. From an early age, Catherine demonstrated a noticeably cool detachment from her surroundings. Her watchful eyes must have let her siblings know their little sister was an unusually gifted child, a sensitive girl whose melancholy personality and precocious intellect clearly set her apart from her privileged peers.

Catherine Fieschi had a considerable capacity for silence. By the age of twelve she had received the gift of prayer; a year later, when other girls anticipated the impending rites of passage accompanying their introduction into the glittering world of Genovese society, Catherine asked to enter a convent — following after her older sister Limbania.

It isn't hard to imagine the hopes and dreams of this thoughtful thirteen-year-old as she reflected upon her sister's entrance into the convent and confided her intentions to her confessor, the convent's chaplain. Nor is it difficult to understand why, for three years in a row, he repeatedly refused Catherine's requests.

"What could a mere child, especially the daughter of one of Genoa's most affluent families, possibly know about the rigorous demands of religious life?" the priest must have wondered. How could he have foreseen what his decision would eventually cost her?

No More World, No More Sins

> *I delight greatly in the Lord; my soul rejoices in my God.* Isaiah 61:10

In the end, Catherine's desire to become a nun was dashed by two family events: The first was the death of her father at the end of 1461. Had he lived, he might have spared Catherine the subsequent ceremony: an arranged marriage negotiated by her eldest brother, Giacomo.

Before Catherine could pursue her dream of entering a religious order, she was "sacrificed" by her family in an attempt to secure peace with their longtime rivals, the Adorno family. Through Catherine's union with Guiliano Adorno, Giacomo believed he could eliminate an old enemy, broadening the Fieschi's economic and political influence.

The feud between the Fieschi and Adorno families sounds like the setting for Shakespeare's *Romeo and Juliet*. Two great families, caught in centuries-old bitter rivalry. But the similarities between literature and real life fall apart when it comes to romance. Unlike Romeo and Juliet, Catherine and Guiliano weren't in love. A disconsolate — and very young fifteen years old — Catherine was wholly unprepared for marriage to a pleasure-seeking, pampered spendthrift with a fiery temper.

For the first five years, Guiliano was rarely at home. Catherine's yearning for a cloistered religious life continued in spite of — or, perhaps, *because* of — her husband's hedonistic lifestyle. Guiliano recklessly spent his fortune and had numerous affairs with other women, including a mistress who gave birth to his child, a daughter named Thobia.

Meanwhile Catherine sank into a deep depression and voluntarily confined herself to her home for about five lonely years. Then, in an attempt to please her family and find some degree of happiness, she resumed her role in the Fieschi's extravagant social life for another five years. It didn't work. Later she would describe the first decade of her marriage as a time of intense personal suffering, for even as she immersed herself in nonstop social activities, Catherine still felt utterly miserable — and alone.

The daily distractions provided by Catherine's packed social calendar drained, rather than replenished, her emotional reserves. Just after Christmas 1472, Catherine's depression deepened, and she desperately prayed to God for divine assistance.

Relief came nearly three months later, on March 22, 1473. At the age of twenty-five, a little more than ten years after her marriage, Catherine knelt for confession; she asked God to send her to bed for three months.

God provided a far better answer to Catherine's drastic plea for help. Two days later, during a visit to her sister's convent, Catherine again felt compelled to go to confession. As she knelt before the chaplain, she was filled with the Holy Spirit, her heart pierced, according to her biographer, "by so sudden and immense a love of God, accompanied by so penetrating a sight of her miseries and sins and of His goodness, that she was near falling to the ground. And in a transport of pure and all-purifying love, she was drawn away from the miseries of the world."[3]

Catherine's new life had begun.

She returned home with one prayer on her lips, a prayer to the God whose love had transformed — and would continue to transform — her life: "O Love, is it possible that you have called me with so much love and have revealed to me in one moment what no tongue can describe?"[4]

God's Love in Action

> *For he has clothed me with garments of salvation and arrayed me in a robe of righteousness, as a bridegroom adorns his head like a priest, and as a bride adorns herself with her jewels.* Isaiah 61:10

From that day on Catherine laid aside the "weight" of her heartache, resentment, and bitterness and lived a prayerful, Christ-centered life that continued until her death in 1510. Her newly discovered faith was accompanied by an intense, lifelong hunger for Holy Communion. At the time, taking Communion every day was not a common practice, yet the Lord provided this unique privilege for Catherine —

without her ever having to ask — through the priests who were inspired by the Holy Spirit to serve her.

In addition to his calling her to a "hidden" life of contemplative prayer and daily Communion, Catherine sensed the Lord urging her toward an additional vocation, working among the destitute on the streets of Genoa and at the vast wards of the Pammatone Hospital. Though her work as a nurse was hardly considered a satisfactory profession for a woman of her social standing, Catherine simply ignored her critics, plunged straight ahead in spite of her own doubts, and grew into her role as a servant of the sick and dying poor. In time, she overcame her natural repulsion of lice-covered heads and pus-filled wounds by directly depending on God's strength — and deliberately taking on the most repellent and distasteful cases.

"To do this work well, love is needed," Catherine later told those who wished to follow her example.[5]

As she started her hospital work, Catherine's marriage underwent a profound change. Guiliano's out-of-bounds lifestyle brought the couple into bankruptcy; they were forced to sell several properties and rent out their palace.

What might have been a particularly humiliating event for these two descendants of Genoa's leading families ended up working for their mutual good. Guiliano turned to Christ — perhaps, in part, because of his wife's courageous example — and eventually took his vows as a lay Franciscan. For reasons never disclosed, he and Catherine agreed to live together celibately, and peacefully, for nearly twenty years until his death.

Though legally bankrupt, Guiliano and Catherine still had an income that could have afforded them a modest, comfortable home. But their faith directed them to relocate to a humble house among the poor, near Pammatone Hospital, where Guiliano invested his life working alongside his wife.

At some point during these early years of their ministry together, Catherine learned about the existence of Guiliano's former mistress and their daughter, Thobia. Motivated by the love of Christ, Catherine reached out to Thobia and to her mother, who later entered a religious order. Catherine's acceptance of this child, combined with her unflinching forgiveness of her husband and his mistress, was a dynamic witness to the Lord's love.

A Fierce — and Fearless — Devotion

> *I will tell of the kindnesses of the Lord, the deeds for which he is to be praised, according to all the Lord has done for us.* Isaiah 63:7

After several years of hard work, in 1479 Catherine and Guiliano quietly gave up their small cottage and moved into a two-room apartment in the hospital. Eleven years later, Catherine was appointed administrator of the massive, 130-bed institution, which also had an orphanage for a hundred girls.

Catherine quickly proved herself a sensible, skilled hospital director — a surprising job for an "otherworldly" kind of person who would later be called a mystic by her many biographers. During her six-year tenure, it is said that her budgets were always balanced. She capably directed her staff even as she cared for the sick and privately pursued an intimate relationship with Christ through prayer.

In 1493, as the plague swept through Europe, many of Genoa's citizens fled to their country homes to avoid infection. Most of the people who stayed behind were too poor to travel. Catherine and Guiliano were among the exceptions.

Pammatone's creative administrator quickly converted a vacant area outside the hospital into a gigantic open-air infirmary covered with billowing white cloths, where she moved from person to person providing spiritual comfort and doing what she could to ease her patients' pain and suffering. This became the indelible image of Catherine that the surviving townspeople would later look back upon and remember.

She and Guiliano courageously remained at their posts, heroically working day and night, in spite of the mortal danger surrounding them. Of those who remained in the city, four out of five perished.

Catherine herself became ill with the plague after kissing a dying woman. Though Catherine recovered slowly, she never regained full health and eventually was forced to resign her post, though she continued to live and work in the hospital. In 1497 Catherine nursed Guiliano through an illness that took his life the year after Catherine left her position.

Widowed at age fifty, Catherine attracted a sizable group of students who shared in her hospital work and listened closely as she spoke about her relationship with the Lord, the love of her life. Often, as Catherine attempted to explain her insights, she exclaimed, "O would that I could tell you how my heart feels!" To which they would eagerly respond, "O Mother, tell us something of it." And then she would simply answer: "I cannot find words appropriate to so great a love. But this I can say with truth, that if of what my heart feels but one drop were to fall into Hell, Hell itself would altogether turn into Eternal Life."[6]

Some of Catherine's spiritual discourses were recorded by her pupils. Two of these extended talks are still counted as classics in Christian literature even though it appears that Catherine herself never wrote down her thoughts or kept a journal.

As Catherine's earthly existence approached its conclusion, her body was broken by poor health and a variety of undiagnosed ailments, causing tremendous physical suffering. Yet she frequently experienced the Holy Spirit's indescribable joy and was sometimes overheard talking with angels. After becoming very ill, she developed a high fever and died on September 15, 1510. Facing death, she was still intensely aware of the love of God, saying, "Love of God . . . Sweetness of God . . . Charity, union, and peace . . . God, God."[7]

Summarizing her life, Robert Ellsberg notes that Catherine "spent much of her days and nights in ardent prayer, in which, it is said, she experienced the burning flame of God's presence in her heart. What is more remarkable, however, is that this contemplative life was not spent in a convent." He continues: "Catherine remained a laywoman, immersed in hands-on nursing care for the sick and dying poor. She helped to found and maintain the first hospital in Genoa, at various times performing every type of work from the most menial to the office of director. It is this extraordinary combination of action and contemplation that has made her one of the most compelling figures in the history of Christian spirituality."[8]

Jesus, Thou Joy of loving hearts,
Thou Fount of life, Thou Light of men,
From the best bliss that earth imparts,
We turn unfilled to Thee again.

Thy truth unchanged hath ever stood,
Thou savest those that on Thee call;
To them that seek Thee, Thou art good,
To them that find Thee, all in all.

We taste Thee, O Thou living Bread,
And long to feast upon Thee still;
We drink of Thee, the Fountainhead,
And thirst our souls from Thee to fill.

Our restless spirits yearn for Thee,
Where'er our changeful lot is cast;
Glad when Thy gracious smile we see,
Blest when our faith can hold Thee fast.

O Jesus, ever with us stay,
Make all our moments calm and bright;
Chase the dark night of sin away,
Shed o'er the world Thy holy light.

— Bernard of Clairvaux (1091–1153)

Conclusion

❧

*D*o you remember the first time you tasted the incomparable sweetness of Jesus' love? Or rested securely inside the rock-solid safety of the Lord's gentle presence? How has the love of Christ helped you? Sustained you? Encouraged you? Strengthened you? If you were to write a love letter to the Lord right now, what would you want to tell him?

It's such a relief to know that we don't have to be perfect to be accepted by God, that there's absolutely nothing we can do to deserve or earn the Lord's love. But the love Jesus gives us is so unlike anything else in our experience that we don't always know how to respond to it.

Isn't it amazing how simple it is to impose limits on God's immeasurable love for us without even realizing what we're doing?

When our Savior's love seems remote, we may occasionally find ourselves discounting his promises as we push ourselves harder and harder to prove that we're worthy of the Lord's acceptance. We may mistakenly think that the love of Christ can be bartered for — earned in exchange for our good works and good behavior. Or we may opt to neglect our need to quietly consider God's great love each day as we rest our hearts and minds in our gentle Shepherd's life-giving presence.

The fact is, the Bible tells us that the Lord's love for us is solid, secure, dependable, and unshakable. Permanent. In other words, *nothing can happen in our lives that will remove us from God's love.*

"Who shall separate us from the love of Christ? Shall trouble or hardship or persecution or nakedness or danger or sword?" the apostle Paul asked the Roman Christians in his epistle. "No, in all these things we are more than conquerors through him who loved us. For I am convinced that neither death nor life, neither angels nor demons, neither the present nor the future, neither height nor depth, nor anything else in all creation, will be able to separate us from the love of God that is in Christ Jesus" (Rom. 8:35, 37–39).

Of this passage, Oswald Chambers explains, "Paul is speaking of the things that might seem likely to separate or wedge in between the saint and the love of God; but the remarkable thing is that nothing *can* wedge in between the love of God and the saint.... The bedrock of our Christian faith is the unmerited, fathomless marvel of the love of God exhibited on the Cross of Calvary, a love we never can and never shall merit. Paul says this is the reason we are more than conquerors in all these things, super-victors, with a joy we would not have but for the very things which look as if they are going to overwhelm us." He then refers to the "undaunted radiance" that is built "on the love of God that nothing can alter."[9]

As we steadily draw closer to Christ, just as the Samaritan woman did when she met Jesus sitting alongside Jacob's well, we are inwardly reassured that his plans and purposes for us are for our good. We see he accepts us in a way that is wonderfully foreign to our earthbound, human experience. Opening our hearts to receive the fullness of his love, as Catherine of Genoa did as a young woman — and as she continued to do, even when she bravely refused to abandon her hospital post as a deadly epidemic swept through her city —

we trust what the Lord tells us no matter how shadowy our surroundings may appear. His love is constant. His grace is near. In her "writings," Catherine noted that God's "grace increases in proportion as man makes use of it. Hence it is evident that God gives man from day to day all that he needs, no more and no less, and to each according to his condition and capacity. All this he does for love."[10]

I started this chapter with a verse, 1 John 4:19: "We love because he first loved us." With confidence I say that in their mature years the Samaritan woman and Catherine of Genoa would have affirmed John's statement. As they opened themselves to God's love, they loved him — and others.

I can think of no higher goal in life than living to love God and, through him, learning how better to love myself and others. If undaunted radiance is the end result of such an effort, that's fine with me. How about you?

Will you believe today that God loves you with an everlasting love and that he is calling you to courageously use the gifts he has given you for his glory?

Will you walk away, step by step, from the false ideals and illusions you may have long believed about love and learn to live with the dependable reality of God's great love for you?

If you were to write a love letter to the Lord right now, what would you want to tell him?

Points for Reflection

1. My understanding of the Lord's love for me grows when ...
2. Because of my experience with human love, I see love as ...
3. Jesus' conversation with the woman at the well reveals ...
4. For me, loving God is best expressed by ...
5. Catherine of Genoa's sacrificial love for Christ helps me realize that ...
6. The choice to actively love Jesus requires ...

Prayer: Lord, awaken my heart to celebrate Your love: shine within me, ignite my spirit, set me all aglow! I cannot love without Your love. Only You can satisfy my deepest needs and revive my spirit; only You can bring life to the desert places in my heart. I thank you, Father, for Your promise to quench my thirst with living water — a fountain of love, a reservoir of peace, a wellspring of joy, for all who call upon Your name. Cause me to drink from Your streams of rejoicing as I place my hope in You alone. In Jesus' name, I pray. Amen.

Your love, O Lord, reaches to the heavens,
your faithfulness to the skies.
Your righteousness is like the mighty mountains,
your justice like the great deep.
O Lord, you preserve both man and beast.
How priceless is your unfailing love!
Both high and low among men
find refuge in the shadow of your wings.
They feast on the abundance of your house;
you give them drink from the river of your delights.
For with you is the fountain of life;
in your light we see light.

— Psalm 36:5–9

To believe in the wide-awake real, through all the stupefying, enervating, distorting dream: to will to wake, when the very being seems athirst for Godless repose: — these are the broken steps up to the high fields where repose is but a form of strength, strength but a form of joy, joy but a form of love.[11]

— George MacDonald (1824–1905)

I sought the Lord, and afterward I knew
He moved my soul to seek him, seeking me;
It was not I that found, O Savior true;
No, I was found of thee.

Thou didst reach forth thy hand and mine enfold;
I walked and sank not on the storm-vexed sea;
'Twas not so much that I on thee took hold,
As thou, dear Lord, on me.

I find, I walk, I love, but O the whole
Of love is but my answer, Lord, to thee;
For thou wert long beforehand with my soul,
Always, thou lovedst me.

— Edward J. Hopkins (1818–1901)

Chapter Three

In Patience

What cannot be done in one year can be done in ten.[1]

— Catherine of Genoa (1447–1510)

Remain in me, and I will remain in you. No branch can bear fruit by itself; it must remain in the vine. Neither can you bear fruit unless you remain in me," Jesus told His disciples shortly before His death. "As the Father has loved me, so have I loved you. Now remain in my love" (John 15:4, 9).

Today Jesus still invites us to enter into his life, patiently abide in his love, remain in his presence on good days and bad, even when we feel utterly unworthy of his approval. "Remain in His presence." It's meant to be our everyday mode of operation rather than an occasional experience, a state of continuous dependence upon the Holy Spirit's sustenance no matter what life brings from moment to moment — a broken promise, a chronic illness, an unexpected family crisis, a phone that never quits ringing.

Remain in me, and I will remain in you. Andrew Murray noted, "He offers himself, the keeper of Israel that slumbers not nor sleeps, with all His power and love, as *the living home of the soul.* These words are no law of Moses, demanding from the sinful what they cannot perform. They are the command of love."[2] These are the wise words of the Teacher attentively training his disciples, the Shepherd diligently watching over his flock, the Bridegroom tenderly sheltering his beloved.

Patiently waiting on the Lord ... abiding in Christ ... courageously enduring each successive season as God causes all things to work together for our good. This is the deeply rooted foundation from where we start, and continue, our growth in Christ. Then, firmly planted, we thrive and bear fruit for the kingdom of God. Good works, spiritual gifts, loving relationships — many of the best things we associate with what it means to be Christ's followers — come out of patiently waiting, abiding, and enduring.

Sometimes the Lord places us in a situation where it almost seems as if we have no other choice but to wait and pay attention to what Jesus wants to teach us. Emily's waiting began with a diagnosis of placenta previa during her fourth pregnancy, a condition that required nearly complete bed rest in the final months before her baby's birth. To prevent uterine bleeding and premature labor, all Emily's usual daily activity — housework, meal preparation, errand running, part-time university work — was off-limits.

"It was so frustrating to be confined to my bed day after day when I could clearly see everything that needed to be done," explains Emily. "Even getting things ready for the baby — the shopping, nursery preparation, and 'nesting' types of things I wanted to do in the last few weeks before the baby arrived — was out of the question. But because I didn't want to do anything that would compromise the baby's health, I followed the doctor's orders and did whatever I could do from my bed.

"There had never been a time in my adult life when I had to stop doing and just sit down for a period of twelve weeks. Twelve weeks! I had a husband, three children, a two-story home, my teaching job, and church-related responsibilities to think about. How was everyone and everything going to be taken care of without me?"

Given her family's needs and her own expectations, Emily initially felt tremendous frustration with the physical limitations of her condition. But as the months passed, she found that her stress level was actually lower. In its place was a growing capacity for patience.

"Now that my children are grown and I look back on those final months of Daniel's prenatal development, I can see in retrospect that it was a unique period that brought about a providential turning point in my life. Until then, I had excelled in the art of packing every possible activity into each waking moment of my existence. I'd always been an overdoer, flying from one task to the next, believing that taking care of others was the most important thing in life. But in those three months, God taught me something new: I learned that sometimes waiting can be much more important than doing."

The choice to wait patiently on God's timing is not often easy, especially when it's all we think we can do to rush to the next appointment, perform the next task, accomplish the next goal. Like Emily, my sister Kerry learned something about waiting when physical illness — chronic fatigue syndrome — slowed her down.

"I had been looking forward to finally being out of school and working at my new job," she recalls. "Suddenly, there was no real possibility of paid employment outside the home for me. I couldn't concentrate. Even driving became difficult, which made the long commute out of the question. This represented a radical change in the direction my life was going in. I had been working in one capacity or another since I was fourteen."

The long hours spent in the serene solitude of her bedroom brought an unexpected bonus for Kerry. She rediscovered the joys and benefits of private prayer, quiet contemplation of God's Word, and frequent fellowship with the Lord. In previous years, her life had been full of academic study and busy social activity. Now Kerry was privileged to have time to develop spiritual strength in an area of her life she had neglected.

"I wouldn't trade the time I've spent with Jesus for anything I might have achieved at the new job. Still, being physically sick has been incredibly challenging," she notes. "Sometimes I just get really sick of being sick. I get discouraged. If it had been totally up to me, this is not the route I would have chosen to take."

Like it or not, our aloneness primes our hearts to receive Christ more fully and intimately as we hear his words, ponder his suffering, examine his wounds. We grow in our understanding of the Holy Spirit's comfort as we look to heaven for help. We start to realize just how far Jesus' unfailing love for us extends past our limited ability to grasp its exceeding greatness.

Remaining in the Lord — abiding in Christ — may seem like a bona fide luxury, given the daily demands placed upon our time, energy, and resources. But we can *choose* to say yes to God. We don't need a physical breakdown or an incapacitating pregnancy to find time to remain in Christ. I give these examples as just that — examples — of how two women first learned the importance of what had previously been missing in their hectic lives.

In his book *Abide in Christ,* Andrew Murray questions a view of the Christian life that insists that we must step out and act before we can "expect God to do His part." He notes how hard it is for people who hold this view "to understand what Scripture means when it speaks of our being still and doing nothing, of our resting and waiting to see the salvation of God." He continues, "It appears to them a perfect contradiction, when we speak of this quietness and ceasing from all effort as the secret of the highest activity of man and all his powers. And yet this is exactly what Scripture does teach."

Murray concludes: "The soul in which the wondrous combination of perfect passivity with the highest activity is most completely realized has the deepest experience of what the Christian life is." He gives high priority to the lesson of "stillness of soul," saying that "in it alone can we cultivate that teachableness of spirit, to which the Lord will reveal His secrets — that meekness to which He shows His ways."[3]

Waiting. Abiding. Worshiping. *Remaining.* These words apply to Anna, a woman briefly introduced in the nativity narrative of the gospel of Luke, a woman who waited and watched in patience for the Messiah's arrival. And they apply to the unusual character known as Mary of Egypt, a woman of the world who renounced her high life for a solitary desert life with the Lord. For these two women, a dynamic blend of courage and patient waiting cultivated their spirits to receive the life-changing counsel of God.

Anna's Story

Anna was a prophetess who never left the Jerusalem temple, Luke says. She stayed there night and day, worshiping, fasting, praying ... waiting for her Messiah (Luke 2:36–38). Luke tells us little else about Anna, but we certainly know this about her: She listened, waited, and watched for God and his work.

In some ways Roman rule had transformed Israel — with armies, taxes, idolatry, and politics. Now more than ever the Jewish people looked for a Messiah, a Savior who would deliver them — whether politically or spiritually.

Yet despite Roman rule, the Jewish people still had their temple — a new temple built by Herod. It was the jewel of Jerusalem, an awe-inspiring symbol of the one true God and the extraordinary nation he had established through Abraham and Isaac. It's said that on a sunny day, the gold and the off-white stone of the temple structure shone so brightly that it hurt one's eyes.

I can hardly imagine the sights, smells, and sounds of that temple: God's chosen people, yes, but also myriads of animals alive and being sacrificed; the smells of burnt flesh mixed with fragrant incense; the prayers and songs and heartfelt "sacrifices of praise."

Much of the temple's "goings-on" was off-limits to women — even to Anna, though she spent years on the grounds. How and why did she get there? The details are sketchy, but there are a few hints.

The Woman Who Refused to Leave

> *As we have heard, so have we seen in the city of the Lord Almighty, in the city of our God: God makes her secure forever. Within your temple, O God, we meditate on your unfailing love.* Psalm 48:8–9

*W*hen Luke introduces us to Anna, she is an old woman. "Very old," Luke says, and then he reveals her age: eighty-four — a respectable age even now, more so then.

Luke gives us a glimpse of Anna's family history: She was the daughter of Phanuel, a descendant of Jacob's son Asher. The tribe of Asher was from Galilee, in the north, which may mean that Anna, in Jerusalem, was separated from her family. She married when young. Like virtually every Jewish bride, she had longed for a child. Seasons of fertility came and went and, alas, she never became pregnant. She had been named after the Old Testament Hannah, the long-barren woman who eventually was mother to the judge Samuel. Like Hannah, she asked God to open her womb. But motherhood wasn't in God's plan for Anna — whose name means "grace." And through these cycles of anticipation and then disappointment, she learned something about patience.

After seven years of marriage, her husband died. (Seven being the perfect number — might this give us a hint that it was a good marriage? I'd like to think so.) Her heart was broken, and in that grief she had choices to make. In her day, a childless widow had few options and would have been dependent on family. A widow might return to her father's household or marry her husband's brother. Anna — a displaced young woman from Galilee — may not have had any family. Or she may have simply chosen the route of radical dedication to and reliance on God.

Eugenia Price said, "Anna permitted her heartbreak to force her to God.... Those of us who have faced tragedy of any kind — particularly those of you who are widows — know that nothing heals the wounds like being consciously with God."[4]

Anna went to the temple in Jerusalem and stayed there. Luke says, "She never left the temple but worshiped night and day, fasting and praying" (2:37). Some scholars say she lived in the temple; some think she slept elsewhere but spent all her waking hours in the house of God. Anna evidently had no official religious role on the temple grounds. As a woman and a widow, she operated within a different spiritual sphere than that of the priests and scribes.

Here, Anna's widowhood was transformed into a fragrant offering to the Most High. Perhaps she slept on a small cot in a solitary cell, as would so many religious women who came after her. Perhaps she spent hours on her knees. In her younger years, perhaps she, like David, danced with delight before her Lord.

Perhaps Isaiah's words fed Anna's soul during the long hours when hunger pangs reminded her that she had not eaten a meal since the previous morning: "Therefore the Lord himself will give you a sign: The virgin will be with child and will give birth to a son, and will call him Immanuel" (Isa. 7:14).

Even as she waited, Anna must have often walked about the temple, teaching the Scriptures as she addressed various groups of women, discretely speaking with a few men in the courtyard, offering her calm assistance to stressed-out visitors from distant cities. She particularly liked Simeon, a devout servant of the Lord who had been told by God he would not see death until he beheld the Messiah with his own eyes. Like her friend Simeon, Anna knew the secret joys and burdens associated with being a Jewish prophet. And when the still small voice of the Spirit spoke to her mind and heart, she chose not to dismiss the silent messages as a figment of her imagination; rather, Anna confidently shared the words as they were given to her by God.

The seasonal crowds came and went — Passover, Pentecost, Purim — year after year. And then there was the daily traffic. Women coming for their purification after childbirth. Babies and families. Priests and scribes. Sometimes she would look over these people, chosen by God, and wonder how he would use them to perform his purposes. And yes, on some cloudy mornings she wondered how he would ever use her, a childless widow, a solitary woman.

The years of her widowhood added up. Soon the years were decades. One. Two. Three. She no longer thought in terms of her widowhood — her loss. Instead she thought in terms of the number of years she had been privileged to abide in the presence of the Lord.

She never looked in a mirror, but from what she could see of her body, she knew she was looking old, growing delicate, the rigors of age and fasting increasingly whittling into the once-soft curves of her face and figure. Her hair, coiled at the nape of her neck, tucked under her veil, was no longer dark brown, but white.

Eventually Anna had spent fifty years in the temple — her jubilee celebration. Sometimes she longed to be taken off this earth, and yet God held her here, for a purpose. And as she waited for that purpose to unfold — and for her Messiah to appear — she continued to worship, remaining patiently faithful to God's plan.

"In reality holiness consists in one thing alone, namely, fidelity to God's plan," noted Jean-Pierre de Caussade, an eighteenth-century French spiritual director. "And this fidelity is equally within everyone's capacity in both its active and passive practice."[5]

The ardent pursuit of God was Anna's abiding passion. While drawing apart from the world may seem a stiflingly dull prospect to many people, it apparently was not a boring or trivial pursuit for Anna: Her secluded temple-bound life allowed her God-given gifts to flourish.

In just a few sentences Luke gives us a picture of a confident, wise, unwavering, articulate woman who is in tune with God.

For This Is God Our God

> *Walk about Zion, go around her, count her towers, view her citadels, that you may tell of them to the next generation. For this God is our God for ever and ever; he will be our guide even to the end.* Psalm 48:12–14

*A*ugustine of Hippo wrote these insightful words about time: "The river of time sweeps on, but there, like a tree planted by the water, is our Lord Jesus Christ. He became man, willing to plant himself by the river of time. If you feel yourself drifting down to the rapids, lay hold of the tree; if you are caught up in the love of the world, hold on to Christ. He for your sake entered into time, but he did not cease to be eternal."[6]

Anna was a woman who knew the meaning of holding on.

One morning in her eighty-fourth year, she said her morning prayers with the same hope that had seen her through every day of the last how many years — she no longer knew for sure. Maybe today would be the day when God would cut through time and reveal himself.

As Anna walked — maybe with a cane — out into the courtyard, she noticed a young couple with a baby standing near a wall. She suddenly felt the familiar tug of the Spirit, the inner prompting to head toward temple visitors who might need her guidance. Only this time, there was a difference. She hesitated. Could it be?

Within moments, she noticed her friend Simeon approaching the demurely veiled woman cradling a baby boy in her arms. Then, from a distance, she heard the phrase she would never forget. "Lord, now I can die in peace!" Simeon cried aloud. "As you promised me, I have seen the Savior you have given to all people. He is a light to reveal God to the nations, and he is the glory of your people Israel!" (Luke 2:29–32 NLB).

Anna gasped, dropped her cane, and raised her hands in praise to the living God as she hobbled toward Simeon, the baby, and his parents. There was an authority in her step that Simeon hadn't seen in years. It was obvious to him that Anna also knew who this baby was.

Anna stepped toward the mother. Then, right then and there, the prophetess broke into spontaneous praise for her Lord. This was the day she'd been awaiting for so long. Her words leapt to life: *"Here he is! Here he is! Here he is! Behold the Son of God — Jesus, our Redeemer! Glory to God in the highest: The Messiah has come to us at last!"*

Anna's faithful witness touched many as "she spoke about the child to all who were looking forward to the redemption of Jerusalem" (v. 38). The fruit of her great patience, her long years of abiding in Christ, was the courageous testimony of telling others of the great news: Her Lord had come!

Mary of Egypt's Story

❧

Second only to suffering, waiting may be the greatest teacher and trainer in godliness, maturity, and genuine spirituality most of us ever encounter," noted Richard Hendrix in *Leadership Journal*.[7]

These words vividly describe Mary of Egypt, one of the most talked about people within the celebrated circle of saints of the Orthodox Church. Mary is believed to have lived in the Jordanian desert for nearly five decades following her dramatic conversion to Christianity. Her unforgettable tale first appeared in a Greek version reliably written by Sophronius, Patriarch of Jerusalem, around A.D. 639. Her story became widely known during the Middle Ages, when numerous translations of her unforgettable tale were available in at least fourteen languages, including English, German, Spanish, and French — a telling indication of Mary's popularity in the West as well as the East.

Long ago — in the fifth century — a daughter named Mary was born into an Egyptian household. For reasons unknown to us, Mary left her parents' home at the age of twelve. Were her parents dead? Was Mary running away from an abusive father, an arranged marriage, indentured servitude? Had she been shunned by her community for socially unacceptable behavior? No documents explain Mary's intentions for us. But trustworthy sources indicate that Mary bypassed marriage and family life to pursue fame and fortune in the big city. That meant Alexandria, a sophisticated port on the Nile

Delta, established and named for the Greek conqueror, where a beautiful young woman could rapidly acquire a substantial fortune as an entertainer and courtesan. In her book *Saint Watching* Phyllis McGinley pointedly says: "Mary of Egypt was a harlot like Magdalene before her."[8]

It seems Mary loved her life, and what a life! Even by today's standards, Mary was a wild child: she claimed to lose her virginity for pleasure, not for money; indulged in whatever sexual acts she found intriguing; captivated her easily targeted conquests in a passionate pursuit of new thrills; and lived luxuriously on the income derived from her work as an adventurous actress.

It isn't difficult to picture a young woman like Mary — lost to her past, oblivious to her future — living the high life in one of the most dazzling cosmopolitan cities the world has ever known.

Surprised by Tears

> *"Come to me with your ears wide open. Listen, for the life of your soul is at stake."* Isaiah 55:3 NLB

*D*uring Mary's era, it is unlikely that people viewed her self-destructive compulsions with any compassionate interest. She was doubtless regarded as "a worldly woman," the kind of companion affluent lovers ardently idolize and never marry. By all accounts, Mary possessed the type of fascinating physical beauty and exquisite sexual allure that provided her paramours with an appealing excuse to break their most sacred promises — not once or twice, but as many times as they believed they could afford it.

Evidently, sex gave Mary what she thought she needed. As soon as the intense satisfaction produced by a romantic encounter began to diminish, the next scheduled (or spontaneous) rendezvous would come along, arousing a new level of excitement. Today, we use a clinician's vocabulary to describe someone like Mary. We define this troubling problem in psychological terms and place a clearly defined label on the person's self-destructive lifestyle. We call it sex addiction.

Early on, perhaps even before her flight to Alexandria, a hard-to-break behavioral pattern was set in motion, habitually trapping Mary in what might have been a permanent way of life. But the Lord Jesus Christ had a wonderfully different plan for Mary's future: he chose to lead her out of the darkness of death into eternal life by the light of his perfect holiness.

One day, almost eighteen years after Mary had left her childhood home, she stood near the coastline watching a good number of men walking down a long pier to a large ship. When she happened to ask one of them where they were going, the man answered simply, "To Jerusalem, for the festival of the Exaltation of the Holy Cross." Who can figure? With that one line, the course of Mary's life was radically redirected.

Mary got on that ship and sailed east. Later, Mary said she boarded because she had been intrigued by the illicit escapades such a trip afforded. She realized she wouldn't need any money to pay for her food and transit fare; her body would be the means of supplying her travel expenses. And she reportedly seduced as many men as possible during the journey.

Whatever prompted her to get on that ship (surely she'd seen hundreds of other ships leave that harbor), once she set foot in Palestine, a spiritual curiosity drew her to accompany the other pilgrims to Jerusalem, to honor the cross at the festival. She stayed and mingled with the crowd surrounding the Church of the Holy Sepulchre even though she had absolutely no idea what the festival was about. An innate inquisitiveness, rather than any kind of religious belief, irresistibly compelled the notorious woman to remain standing at the sacred site.

Or so she thought. As Mary pushed her way through the crowd toward the church doors, an invisible force firmly pressed Mary back, preventing her entry to the building. Confused, she could do nothing but stand back in the courtyard and watch the worshipers as they crowded into the sanctuary.

No Turning Back

> *Seek the Lord while you can find him. Call on him now while he is near. Let the people turn from their wicked deeds. Let them banish from their minds the very thought of wrongdoing! Let them turn toward the Lord that he may have mercy on them. Yes, turn to our God, for he will abundantly pardon.* Isaiah 55:6–7 NLB

*T*here, standing before the Church of the Holy Sepulchre, Mary was abruptly awakened to her inner brokenness and spiritual poverty. Suddenly aware of her separation from God, she wondered if those invisible hands had prevented her from entering the church because of her self-centered lifestyle.

There, standing on Jerusalem's most holy ground, Mary started to weep loudly. Her beautifully dressed body shook with heavy sobs, bursting a long-accumulated deep reservoir of emotional anguish. *What is happening to me? I feel so empty ... so tired ... so alone.* Passersby stared at her. She didn't care. She just had to get clean. Make peace with God.

When Mary finally looked up, she saw a radiantly beautiful icon of Jesus' mother. The quiet purity reflected in the portrait profoundly touched the pilgrim's heart. Lifting her eyes to heaven, Mary was then and there converted to Christ.

"When I had drunk the spirit of Heaven, and the second birth had restored me so as to make me a new man then immediately in a marvelous manner doubts began to be resolved, closed doors to be opened, dark places to be light," declared Cyprian of Carthage, an early bishop and martyr from North Africa. "What before was difficult now seemed easy."[9]

And so it was for the penitent Mary of Egypt who, from that time on, wholly committed her life to God and walked with Christ.

We can happily imagine what that moment must have been like for Mary as God placed his sovereign hand upon her heart, breathed new life into every part of her being, and permanently transformed her with the glorious power of his immutable love. To say only that Mary experienced a radical life change or some strange spiritual awakening fails to explain what happened to her on that day. Mary's head-to-toe renascence, a rebirth of the most marvelous kind, was nothing short of miraculous.

Before leaving the church property, Mary heard a voice giving her direction: "If you cross over the Jordan, you will find solace and rest."

In response Mary headed east, toward the river. On her way a Christian gave her three loaves of bread. By sundown, she reached the river and washed her face, symbolically washing away the sin and the tears of repentance. She entered the shoreline Church of John the Baptist, where she received the Lord's Supper for the first time. She ate half of the three loaves of bread and drank water from the river.

Mary left for the wilderness the following morning, led across the Jordan by the Holy Spirit. Mary never again returned to civilization.

Considering her former life in Alexandria, how could Mary possibly have "left everything" to go live as a solitary in the desert? What about her fabulous wardrobe? Her extensive investments? How would she eat? What would she eat? Where would she sleep? What about the wind and the wild animals? It seems the questions did not faze Mary who was steadfastly sure she was being called to forsake her former life and turn to God.

Mary may not have known the story of Anna, dedicating her life to God — "worshiping night and day, fasting and praying" — and yet Mary in one sense was following her example, turning to what would be a long, solitary apprenticeship in the presence of her Lord.

A New Creation

> *"My thoughts are completely different from yours," says the Lord. "And my ways are far beyond anything you could imagine. For just as the heavens are higher than the earth, so are my ways higher than your ways and my thoughts higher than your thoughts."* Isaiah 55:8–9 NLB

It is nearly impossible for us to picture Mary's life after she entered the desert's arid, unpopulated, expansive domain. Even so, Sophronius's account gives us a few hints of what happened to her there as she patiently waited upon God and communed with him day after day — for forty-seven years.

Mary's clothes eventually wore out. Her hair grew so long that it covered her darkly tanned naked body. She lived in a cave and ate only berries, tubers, dates, and herbs. Though the Lord's desert-bound disciple could not read, she was schooled in her faith by the Holy Spirit.

We might have known nothing of Mary's devout life if it weren't for a humble desert monk named Zosimus — a hermit much esteemed for his virtuous life and sincerity of repentance. Zosimus had lived a strictly disciplined spiritual life for fifty-three years, since childhood. Wondering if there might be someone who exceeded him in spiritual fervor, he entered the monastery at St. John the Baptist Church on the Jordan — Mary's last stop before crossing the river. (Surely he would find such a person there.)

One spring, when the time arrived for the monastery monks to make their annual Lenten retreat to fast and pray in the desert, Zosimus went alone, across the river, into the desert, where he walked for twenty days before he saw someone in the distance. As the desert was known as a habitation of demons, he made the sign of the cross before heading toward the white-haired, dark-skinned figure. "Stop," he cried.

And Mary — now more than seventy-five years old — did just that. She stopped. What's more she called the stranger by name and then asked him to cover her naked body with his cloak. Before speaking they prostrated themselves before one another: Mary, because she respected the holiness of Zosimus's vocation; Zosimus, because he believed Mary to be a saint.

How did Mary know his name? Zosimus sensed that she was indeed a vessel of the Holy Spirit. Zosimus stayed long enough to hear Mary's story and realized that God's hand was upon her life. Here's what she told him:

> I was born in Egypt. At twelve, leaving my parents' house, I went to Alexandria where, for seventeen years, I gave myself up to a dissolute life. My perversity

became such that meeting some young Libyans, who were going to be present at the Exaltation of the Cross, I embarked with them to seduce them. I seduced them all to the last one. Arrived at the Holy City I wished to take part in the feast and joined the crowd going to the temple, but I found it impossible to cross the threshold and I remained rooted on the spot. Light came to me that it was my crimes that prevented me from entering.... "Cross Jordan," a voice told me, "and you will find peace." After receiving the sacraments of confession and Communion, I crossed the Jordan, and pushed on to this place. Here I have been for forty-seven years, without meeting any human being, eating roots and herbs, and only speaking with God.[10]

"When I think from what evils the Lord has freed me," Mary confessed, "I am nourished by incorruptible food, and I cover my shoulders with the hope of my salvation. I feed upon and cover myself with the Word of God, who contains all things."[11] Having said that, she admitted missing the fish and the wine of Egypt.

Zosimus was amazed at Mary's knowledge of Scripture — repeating verses seemingly by rote — when she'd had no one but God to teach her. He had thought he would find his devout mentor at St. John the Baptist monastery, but the example of holiness turned out to be Mary — a former Egyptian courtesan who had lived for decades in the desert as a valiant spiritual champion of Jesus Christ.

After she shared her life story with Zosimus, Mary asked him not to repeat what she had told him. She also requested that he return one year later, on Maundy Thursday, so that she might be served the Lord's Supper. He went back after a year. But on a third visit, he found only Mary's lifeless body in the sand, wearing the cloak he had given her.

Grieving and wanting to give Mary a proper burial, Zosimus tried as best he could to dig a grave. And here the story grows to supernatural proportions: As the monk prepared for the burial, a mighty lion — "which contemporary audiences would have recognized as a symbol of Christ, the lion of Judah," observes poet Kathleen Norris — appeared to help Zosimus by digging, and then filling, with its paws the grave for Mary of Egypt.[12]

Remaining in Faith

> *"The rain and the snow come down from the heavens and stay on the ground to water the earth. They cause the grain to grow, producing seed for the farmer and bread for the hungry. It is the same with my word. I send it out, and it always produces fruit. It will accomplish all I want it to, and it will prosper everywhere I send it."* Isaiah 55:10–11 NLB

Though Mary of Egypt's story may seem hard for us to grasp, she was not alone in her isolated spiritual journey — she was actually part of a much larger body of believers who lived as hermits in Syria, Egypt, and Palestine during the fourth and fifth centuries.

Like Mary of Egypt, the women who joined this movement discarded their former identities and took up rigorous forms of self-denial as a way of expressing their fervent devotion to Christ. "Desert mothers" subsisted on little food and wore rough, plain, monk-like clothing as a form of protection; in these robes these solitary women were often mistaken for men and less vulnerable to attack by strangers. The women lived solely to serve Christ and his body through focused worship, prayer, and fasting as they followed a calling that kept them completely apart from the world as they expectantly waited for the coming of Christ.

When I read about the "desert mothers" of this experimental era of church history, I'm amazed at how many women chose this lifestyle — living alone in the harsh environment. According to Palladius, a bishop at the turn of the fifth century who lived alone for a while in the Egyptian desert, there were eventually as many as *twenty thousand* desert mothers. Twenty thousand! That's estimated to be nearly twice that of the desert fathers.

Isn't this incredible? What motivated the desert mothers to take such a shockingly radical step of faith? And why did they believe that living as hermits in the middle of the desert was preferable to living for Christ somewhere else?

Pondering Mary's Story — a Historical Perspective

"You will live in joy and peace. The mountains and hills will burst into song, and the trees of the field will clap their hands! Where once there was thorns, cypress will grow. Where briers grew, myrtle will sprout up." Isaiah 55:12–13 NLB

For the desert mothers, living in solitude meant remaining hidden from the world. Like Anna living in the temple, these dedicated women pursued a demanding, spiritually focused life as they patiently stayed attentive to the Lord through their night-and-day practice of worship, prayer, and fasting.

"The desert mothers and fathers were women and men who withdrew themselves from the manipulations of a power-hungry society to fight against evil and grow closer to God in the barrenness of the desert," writer Jill Evans explains. "The world they left behind was lukewarm in its spirituality and full of compromise, much as the world is today. They humbly dedicated themselves as witnesses of the crucified and risen Lord in a life of silent prayer, manual work, solitude and fasting. Whilst others saw possessions as all important, they gave up all to become daughters of God."[13]

From the perspective of our life experience, such a harsh existence seems unnecessary. We fully believe God's grace is sufficient for us. We don't go to ascetic extremes to express our devotion to Christ. We live in the world even as we try not to be of it. We find it difficult to understand why any woman — let alone twenty thousand — would genuinely be led by the Holy Spirit into the desert to remain isolated, hungry, and watching for Christ's second coming for an entire lifetime.

Still, it happened: The Lord blessed these lovable desert disciples with his protection, wisdom, sustenance, and steady companionship as they faithfully followed the radical call of Jesus as the Holy Spirit led them to understand it. The women dwelling in the wilderness were never alone because God was always with them.

"These were simple, practical men [and women], not given either to mysticism or to theology, living by the Word of God, the love of the brethren and of all creation, waiting for the coming of the kingdom with eager expectation, using each moment as a step in their pilgrimage of the heart towards Christ," notes Benedicta Ward, a lecturer at Oxford University.[14]

"It was because of this positive desire for the Kingdom of heaven which came to dominate their whole lives that they went without things: they kept silence, for instance, not because of a proud and austere preference for aloneness but because they were learning to listen to something more interesting than the talk of men, that is, the Word of God," explains Ward. "[They] were rebels, the ones who broke the rules of the world which say that property and goods are essential for life ... that no one can be fully human without sex and domesticity."[15]

I see these exceptionally dedicated Christians as having made a significant impact on human history — given their unimpeded praise of God, strenuous engagement in spiritual warfare, and constant intercession on behalf of Christ's body in the world. Many people — clergy and laypeople alike — went out and sought spiritual direction from the desert mothers and fathers, finding the disciples' radiant faith a refreshing contrast to the scorched wilderness in which they lived.

The King of love my Shepherd is,
Whose goodness faileth never;
I nothing lack if I am His
And He is mine forever.

Where streams of living water flow
My ransomed soul He leadeth,
And where the verdant pastures grow
With food celestial feedeth.

In death's dark vale I fear no ill
With Thee, dear Lord, beside me;
Thy rod and staff my comfort still,
Thy cross before to guide me.

And so thru all the length of days
Thy goodness faileth never:
Good Shepherd, may I sing Thy praise
Within Thy house forever.

— Henry W. Baker (1821–1877)

Conclusion

❧

"If we hope for something we do not see," Guerric of Igny, a twelfth-century monk, explained, "then we exercise patience in waiting."[16]

Anna and Mary spent decades learning the lessons of patient, courageous worship and communion with God — being spiritually shaped through their deep intimacy with God. Yet there certainly must have been moments when each of these women wondered: *How much longer must I wait, O Lord? How much longer?*

And in our fast-paced world today, we are even more impatient. "We want it now. All of it. Whatever it might be," author Michael Downey sagely points out. "Results. Plans realized. Goals achieved. Dreams come true. Supper on the table. Language mastered. Skills acquired. An answer to that letter. Or fax. And we want our prayers answered, too. If there is no answer to our prayers, then why bother with God? What's the point? If God is not useful, if God does not help us out, then why waste our time and energy?"[17]

Scripture makes it clear over and over again — that God's ways are not our ways and God's timing is not our timing. Here's one example. The Lord is talking to his people through the prophet Isaiah: "Why do you say . . . 'My way is hidden from the Lord; my cause is disregarded by my God'? Do you not know? Have you not heard? The Lord is the everlasting God, the Creator of the ends of the earth . . . and his understanding no one can fathom. He gives strength to the weary and increases the power of the weak" (Isa. 40:27–29).

Let me return to Anna's story for a moment. As Anna waited for God to act in a dramatic way in her life — for her people — she "worshiped night and day." For us this may not mean cloistering ourselves away from the world. In his first letter to the Thessalonians, Paul spends considerable time talking about time and the future and the Lord's second coming. And he tells us how to wait — even as we continue to live active lives in the world: "Be joyful always; pray continually; give thanks in all circumstances, for this is God's will for you in Christ Jesus" (1 Thess. 5:16–18).

This kind of waiting — whether for the coming of the Lord or for an answer to a desperate prayer — is not passive. It calls for a courageous and active abiding in Christ: For practical perseverance in applying age-old methods of faith-building as we memorize Scriptures, read psalms, pray or sing a Scripture song upon first waking, before getting out of bed. For discovering, day upon day, year upon year, how and why these spiritual disciplines strengthen our spirits and steady our souls.

"O my God, Trinity whom I adore, let me entirely forget myself that I may abide in you, still and peaceful as if my soul were already in eternity; let nothing disturb my peace nor separate me from you," said Elizabeth of the Trinity, a French Carmelite nun, in the eighteenth century. "O my unchanging God, but that each moment may take me further into the depths of your mystery."[18]

Though we cannot fully understand the mystery of Jesus' help and the Holy Spirit's sustenance as we walk through life on this side of heaven, we can choose: to patiently abide in Christ for the remainder of our lives, as Anna and Mary chose to do; to sit at Jesus' feet, quietly listening for his Word in the midst of a discordant chorus of competing voices; to wait on the Lord to renew our strength — before our own strength runs out; to call upon God for direction — especially when the way ahead is unclear; to pray "Thy will be done" as we lift our tear-stained hands in solitary gratitude to the only One who sees our hearts, bears our grief, feels our suffering, knows our needs, and understands our failures.

Remember this about patience: "What cannot be done in one year can be done in ten" (Catherine of Genoa).

Points for Reflection

1. I am most aware of my need to remain in God's Word when ...
2. Yielding, trusting, and waiting become more difficult when I choose to ...
3. Anna's story caused me to think about ...
4. When I thought about Mary of Egypt living a solitary life as Christ's follower in the desert, I pictured her ...
5. Patient waiting is made more bearable if I ...

Prayer: Dear Father, help me to be patient as I learn to trust You more. Forgive me for allowing my life to become so busy that I am too tired or distracted to spend enough time alone with You. Thank you, Lord, for making me lie down in green pastures, for leading me beside the still waters, for restoring my soul — even when my own preference leads me in a different direction. My desire is to remain with You always, Jesus. Amen.

Hear my cry, O God;
listen to my prayer.

From the ends of the earth I call to you,
I call as my heart grows faint;
lead me to the rock that is higher than I.
For you have been my refuge,
a strong tower against the foe.

I long to dwell in your tent forever
and take refuge in the shelter of your wings.

— Psalm 61:1–4

Patience is more than endurance. A saint's life is in the hands of God like a bow and arrow in the hands of an archer. God is aiming at something the saint cannot see, and He stretches and strains, and every now and again the saint says — "I cannot stand any more." God does not heed. He goes on stretching till His purpose is in sight, then He lets fly.[19]

— Oswald Chambers

Only silently resigned
To the counsels of Thy mind;
Willing, yet rejoicing not,
That Thy purpose shall be wrought.

Is this truly to submit?
Folding placid hands, to sit,
While innumerable feet
Thy triumphant coming meet?

Shall we say, "Thy will be done,"
And on our own errands run?
Vain and evil the design
We pursue apart from Thine.

Teach us how to live this prayer;
Reverently Thy plans to share;
More than echoes of Thy voice,
Make us partners in Thy choice.

Lift us up to catch from Thee
World-encircling sympathy;
Ardor, strength, and courage give;
As Thou livest, let us live.

Let our deeds be syllables
Of the prayer our spirit swells;
In us Thy desire fulfill;
By us work Thy gracious will.

— Lucy Larcom, 1893

Chapter Four

With Humble Confidence

The proud man who trusts in himself may fear to undertake anything, but the humble are bold in proportion to the insufficiency of their own which they feel. As they acknowledge their weakness they acquire strength, because they rely on God.[1]

— Francis de Sales (1567–1622)

I have not done an exhaustive study, but I don't think there are many verses repeated three times in Scripture. Yet one proverb is quoted by both Peter and James: "God opposes the proud but gives grace to the humble" (see Prov. 3:34; James 4:6; 1 Peter 5:5).

I'm not sure most of us know what humility really is, maybe because its root word *humble* is used in two different ways.

Frederick Buechner says, "True humility doesn't consist of thinking ill of yourself but of not thinking of yourself much differently from the way you'd be apt to think of anybody else."[2] Dag Hammarskjöld expressed this definition well when he wrote, "Humility is just as much the opposite of self-abasement as it is of self-exaltation. To be humble is *not to make comparisons.*"[3]

By this definition the humble person sees herself as being one among many — a member of a community. A humble Christian sees herself as a sinner saved by grace, unique and yet one among many, not the "favorite child" with special privileges. As Paul said in Romans 12:3, "Do not think of yourself more highly than you ought, but rather think of yourself with sober judgment, in accordance with the measure of faith God has given you." Paul goes on to talk about the various diverse gifts given to members of the church.

William Temple, archbishop of Canterbury early in the twentieth century, connected this form of humility with confidence: "Real humility makes for effectiveness because it delivers a man from anxiety," which he called "the chief source of feebleness." He illustrated this by describing someone playing catch with a ball. If you're anxious about your performance — *will I catch it? will I? what will everybody think if I don't?* — you'll probably drop the ball. "But if you just catch it without thinking about anything but catching it — not, above all, of what other people are going to think of you — probably you will hold it."[4]

By not unduly worrying about yourself, you're free to walk with confidence — with quiet and courageous confidence.

By another definition of the root word *humble*, we may describe someone, maybe even ourselves, as being humbled — brought down, shamed. This is more closely associated with humiliation than with humility.

But sometimes the two uses of the word are applicable to one person. Sometimes the most humble people have been humbled by harsh circumstances, maybe unjustly imposed by others, maybe prompted or aggravated by a weakness of their own. Humbled people know they sometimes drop that ball — maybe because the sun was blinding them, maybe because they miscalculated. Turning from baseball to the spiritual realm, humble people acknowledge their weaknesses; they know, as the psalmist said, they are made of dust (Ps. 103:14) and acknowledge their dependence on God.

When we admit our vulnerability and acknowledge our weakness, humility provokes us to look *up*.

I see humility in the psalmist who wrote, "I lift up my eyes to the hills — where does my help come from?" (Ps. 121:1). He immediately answered the question: "My help comes from the Lord, the Maker of heaven and earth" (v. 2).

Knowing where our help comes from becomes a matter of faith when familiar signposts disappear and we suddenly find ourselves in a foreign place, soberly seeking God's guidance.

Not long ago, my friend Sharon talked to me about painful experiences she had endured as a pastor's wife. She confessed she was finding it hard to love God as well as to love others. In fact, Sharon has been hurt so deeply by people that she has serious doubts about the Lord's care and concern for her.

As Sharon's story unfolded, I could empathize. After years of Christian service, her faith had faltered following the loss of many of her lifelong ideals. Her husband's unsuccessful public forays into new avenues of ministry had left her feeling burned out and cynical, while their private marital problems had wounded her soul.

"It hurts too much for me to think God loves me and yet has chosen not to protect me in my marriage and church relationships," Sharon confided. "I don't understand what has happened. I feel like I did everything I could do to be a good wife and mom, a good Christian. But that doesn't seem to matter at all now. My life is falling apart."

I listened without attempting to offer my friend any easy answers, mainly because there were none. I thought about the heartbreaks, disappointments, and losses Sharon had encountered over twenty years and wished I could administer a soothing dose of faith that would take the pain away and strengthen her resistance to self-pity, restlessness, revenge, bitterness, and remorse. I wanted to say, *Sharon, Jesus loves you*, and know that she would believe it with her whole heart.

I listened and grieved with her and silently prayed that this injustice and weakness — her pain and in one sense her private humiliation — would bring her to the kind of humility that Peter describes: "Humble yourselves, therefore, under God's mighty hand, that he may lift you up in due time" (1 Peter 5:6).

When rugged circumstances cause the ground beneath us to feel as if the earth is going to slip away, when we know for certain that we cannot stand up by ourselves any longer, when we know we don't have enough wisdom or strength to cope with our current situation, where will we look for help?

Not surprisingly, if our usual coping skills cease working, we're more likely to listen to God. As we wait to hear the Shepherd's next set of instructions, we may discover that the same voice that says "Come unto me" begins to sound much sweeter in the midst of our failure, pain, or loss — when the uncontrollable nature of change transforms our world and causes us to scan the horizon, to look up beyond the hills.

In the ancient story of Queen Esther, we find an example of a woman who knew great humiliation and yet, by humbly turning to the Lord as her source of strength and confidence, she became one of the most noteworthy and courageous women in the Bible. Queen Esther was ready, with God's help and because of his leading, to take the consequences for a bold political action.

And so was a contemporary woman, Rosa Parks, who, like Esther, humbly identified with a group of people being unjustly treated. The two stories have much in common: Ethnic hatred. Legal injustice. Spiritual valor. Civil disobedience. Supernatural strength. Deliverance from racial oppression. Quiet faith. Courageous choices. God's sovereign selection of national heroes. In both stories, a quiet confidence set in motion events that would change the course of history.

Esther's Story

What was it like to be a gorgeous Jewish woman living in the Persian empire during King Xerxes' reign? Such a dangerous experience is nearly impossible for us to imagine as we look back across the centuries to a distant time so far removed from our own age that it seems like it might have never happened at all.

When we think about Esther, we picture a ravishing raven-haired beauty akin to the stunning women featured in magazines or on film. Then we fine-tune our imaginations by considering the story's time frame (about 480 B.C.), the Persian empire's global position (an immense arid region located between Pakistan and the Sudan), and Esther's shifting social status (orphan to adopted daughter to slave to member of the king's harem to queen to national hero).

One of the best things about Esther's story — about all of the Bible's stories, for that matter — is that we always see and learn more over time as we periodically study each character. Our understanding deepens with the changing seasons. We catch hints of new shades of meaning, subtle signs that God has something more to tell us as he keeps calling us back to the same familiar chapters. As we return once more to Esther's world, what insights will we gain from taking a closer look at her timeless beauty?

King Xerxes' Audacious Order

> *Remember, O Lord, your great mercy and love, for they are*
> *from of old.* Psalm 25:6

In 483 B.C., beginning in the third year of his reign, King Xerxes, the powerful ruler of a vast empire spanning from India to Ethiopia, gave a six-month-long banquet for all his princes, courtesans, and governmental officials at the fortified acropolis of Susa, the winter residence of the Persian kings. The event provided the party-loving king with a perfect opportunity to display his impressive wealth as he prepared for a possible war against Greece.

After the full-blown feast, another festive dinner was held. Here all the king's imperial officials and servants were invited to the weeklong event in the courtyard of the palace garden. Even Susa's townspeople were included in the royally sponsored revelry.

The courtyard, adorned with immense marble pillars and a mosaic pavement inlaid with expensive stones, was spread with the best gourmet foods. Free wine for all, though no one could be compelled to consume *more* wine than he wanted. And the wine was served in intricately designed, one-of-a-kind goblets handcrafted of solid gold.

The feast was for men only. King Xerxes' favorite conjugal partner, Queen Vashti, held her own banquet in a different part of the palace, where the wives, sisters, daughters, and mothers of the king's guests were protected from the men's inebriated and embarrassing carousing. Queen Vashti, it turns out, was wise as well as beautiful. She knew the value of boundaries that are worth keeping, regardless of the cost.

On the last day of the banquet, the intoxicated king asked seven of his personal servants — all eunuchs — to bring Queen Vashti, adorned with her royal crown, to the court-yard so that he could show her off. When the queen was told to place the crown upon her uncovered head and openly display her physical beauty before a citywide gathering of ine-briated men, she flatly refused. The request was obscene — a scandalous marital maneuver given the raw judicial power of the king's royal command.

Fuming with anger at being rebuffed — by his own wife — King Xerxes summoned his top astrological advisers. "According to the law, what must be done with Queen Vashti?" the agitated monarch inquired. "She has not obeyed the command of King Xerxes that the eunuchs have taken to her" (Est. 1:15).

A man named Memucan stepped forward, claiming the queen had offended every nobleman in the empire. "For the Queen's conduct will become known to all women, and so they will despise their husbands and say, King Xerxes commanded Queen Vashti to be brought before him, but she would not come. This very day the Persian and Median women of the nobility who have heard about the queen's conduct will respond to all the king's nobles in the same way. There will be no end of disrespect and discord" (Est. 1:17–18).

Memucan proposed the king issue a royal decree, writing it into the laws of Persia and Media, with no possibility of repeal, forbidding Vashti ever again to enter King Xerxes' presence. And why not give Vashti's queenship to another, better woman? "Then when the king's edict is proclaimed throughout all his vast realm, all the women will respect their husbands, from the least to the greatest" (Est. 1:20).

The king took Memucan's advice. He issued the decree. With his most desirable lover permanently banished from his sight, the king soon regretted what he had done. But it was too late. Once King Xerxes had sealed and issued the decree, it was unalterably binding.

An Imperial Abuse of Power

> *He guides the humble in what is right and teaches them his way.* Psalm 25:9

*W*hen King Xerxes' attendants saw the gloom descend upon him after Vashti's departure, they made a suggestion: *Let's find a new queen. The king's agents in each province should search for beautiful young virgins. They should be brought into the royal harem. Hegai, the eunuch in charge of the harem, can give them all beauty treatments. Then the virgin who best pleases the king can be named queen.*

This caught the king's attention. And brought young Esther, or Hadassah, into the story. Hadassah, an orphan, had been raised by her cousin Mordecai. They were Jews living in a foreign land.

Like a highly prized animal, Hadassah was rounded up with countless other young women throughout the empire in a systematic search for royal concubines, suddenly cut off from her comfortable home and prospects for marriage, and forcibly placed in an elite stable of women created and maintained exclusively for the purpose of satisfying the king's socially sanctioned appetites.

She was not courted by the king. Her arrival at the palace in Susa was not the result of a royal romance. Forced to become a concubine in Persia's most famous harem, she lost two of the most precious things that belong to a woman: her name — from Hadassah to Esther — and her virginity.

How many of us have ever made a realistic assessment of Esther's plight? Her silent suffering? Her one-way ticket to enslavement?

Perhaps we lose track of Esther's anguish because we are caught off guard by her beauty. We prefer to imagine this lovely woman was spared the humiliation of her less fortunate counterparts. Maybe we fool ourselves into believing the king's hunt for women was a beauty contest, with scores of eager contestants seeking the first-place prize. We like to think that Esther *volunteered*.

But Esther did not volunteer. King Xerxes was an imperial ruler, not a celebrity judge. He played for keeps. Once she entered his harem, a concubine's pampered existence revolved around the king's prodigious love life until he grew tired of sleeping with her, which might be after the first time, on their "wedding night." But once in the royal harem, a concubine could never again live outside the palace walls, whether her sexual status was active, on hold, or retired.

By choosing not to romanticize Esther's brutal experience, we honor Hadassah — the Jewish maiden no doubt promised to a prominent Jewish man, the unsophisticated adolescent who knew sacred Scriptures by memory and faithfully celebrated the weekly Sabbath before her departure for King Xerxes' heavily guarded fortress. The person we never have the opportunity to meet or grieve for in this historic account is Hadassah — the carefree, innocent girl Esther once was — who has vanished from the story.

Singled Out — and Chosen

> *Who, then, is the man that fears the Lord? He will*
> *instruct him in the way chosen for him.* Psalm 25:12

*A*s the king's carriage transported the young woman up the road from Mordecai's house, her eyes took in the immense, imposing structure at the top of the hill. She suddenly found it difficult to breathe, as if she were suffocating.

With her eyes closed, Esther silently repeated the words she had memorized long ago with Mordecai's help. "Hear, O Israel: The Lord our God, the Lord is one. Love the Lord your God with all your heart and with all your soul and with all your strength" (Deut. 6:4).

Remember well what the Lord your God did to Pharaoh and to all Egypt. You saw with your own eyes the great trials, the miraculous signs and wonders, the mighty hand and outstretched arm, with which the Lord your God brought you out. The Lord your God will do the same for all the peoples you now fear. Moreover, the Lord your God will send the hornet among them until even the survivors who hide from you have perished. Do not be terrified by them, for the Lord your God, who is among you, is a great and awesome God. (Deuteronomy 7:18–21)

With new strength, she thought of her cousin Mordecai, not herself. *His face looked so old and weary when I looked back at him as the horses drew me away.... With the Lord's help, I will not be afraid. I will remember, Mordecai, my father. I will never forget what you have taught me. I will never forget who I am. I will never forget: "the Lord our God, the Lord is one."*

It was an unspoken phrase — a pure statement of faith — that Esther would repeat again and again to herself in the coming weeks and years.

At the palace gates, Esther noticed something peculiar: the guards gazed at her. *How odd,* Mordecai's protégé thought to herself. *Why do the king's men look at me that way?*

Being ogled was a new experience for the naive girl who had led a sheltered life, protected by the scriptural precepts, precise Levitical health codes, and high moral standards prescribed by Jewish tradition. No one had even hinted to Esther that she was sexually desirable. People had never discussed her beauty. It just wasn't something anyone ever talked about. Not even her intended mate was allowed to praise Esther's breathtaking allure.

The young virgin, completely unaware of the mesmerizing power of her extraordinary loveliness, had no clue of the extraordinary effect she was about to have on Hegai, the head of the harem.

On Firm Footing

> *The Lord confides in those who fear him: he makes his covenant known to them.* Psalm 25:14

Esther managed not to stumble as she stepped from the carriage and followed a servant into her new quarters. She shuddered to think about what her life outside the Jewish community would be like. Esther entered a world where Hebrew laws had no meaning. She prayed God would understand why she had to keep her Jewish identity a secret and abandon the special dietary and health practices of her people.

Over the next twelve months, Esther's cultural assimilation continued in the hands of expert beauty consultants, clothing designers, and sex counselors — transforming the girl into a pleasing partner for the king. Her hair was dyed, cut, and styled to fit the current Susa fashion. Her modest clothes were replaced with a tantalizing, tailor-made wardrobe from the top designers in town. Her face was carefully painted with plant-based eyeliner, lipstick, and other popular cosmetics. Her already perfect skin was slathered day after day with thick aromatic oil and pricey perfume. By the time this twelve-month "beautification" process was completed, Esther no longer looked, sounded, moved — or smelled — like her former self.

But Esther's beauty wasn't skin deep. Within her soul lay a deep reservoir of righteousness.

With genuine humility, Esther asked the Lord to fill her daily with his peace, strength, holiness, and truth. She sought God's help to stay firm in hope, to remain steadfast under oppression, to be protected from harm and evil, to never surrender to Israel's enemies.

Little things brought great encouragement. The eunuch Hegai took a strong liking to her as soon as she arrived — in Esther's estimation a sure sign of God's providential provision. As harem manager, he lavished delicious food and other special privileges upon her, believing her to have the best chance of capturing the king's heart.

Esther felt the Lord's presence wherever she went. She knew God was preparing a way for her as she walked toward the gathering darkness.

Esther Receives the Crown

*My eyes are ever on the Lord, for only he will release my
feet from the snare.* Psalm 25:15

As time passed, Esther had greater understanding of her
situation: She would eventually have to sleep with the
alien King Xerxes. Wise beyond her years, Esther knew
there was no escaping the end for which she had been
inducted into the royal harem, save death.

Like Mordecai, Esther believed God to be bigger than
her situation. *Who knows?* Esther wondered. *How can I, or
anyone else, say with absolute certainty that the Lord our God
won't use my present circumstances to benefit my family and my
people?*

A year after her arrival at the palace, Esther went to the
king's suite. Knowing it would be better to live as a queen
than a concubine, she followed Hegai's advice to the letter:
how to act, what to wear, when to leave. After silently saying
a prayer, she quietly followed Hegai to the king.

As the door closed firmly on Esther's youth, another
opened to adulthood. That night she won the king's overwhelming favor. Esther, this stunning beauty, would be
queen. A holiday was proclaimed; royal gifts distributed;
taxes eased. The empire's heavy hand lifted from the backs
of Esther's people, at least for a moment.

Mordecai's Troubles

> *Turn to me and be gracious to me, for I am lonely and*
> *afflicted. The troubles of my heart have multiplied; free me*
> *from my anguish.* Psalm 25:16–17

*F*or five years Esther lived in a second harem for the king's wives. It seemed as if Esther disappeared into an easy, pampered royal domesticity, far removed from the daily struggles of Susa's less fortunate people.

But we must not forget: Esther was a devout Jew and her identity was still a secret. Though queen, she was unable to leave the palace at will, prevented from practicing her own religion. What's more, she lived knowing that Xerxes continued to sleep with scores of other women. Her entire existence revolved around the choleric king's sexual preferences and peccadilloes.

King Xerxes' queen, however, had a hidden source of human help — Cousin Mordecai, her stepfather since childhood, who providentially had been appointed as a palace official after uncovering a conspiracy to assassinate the king. From a distance, Esther continued to follow her guardian's orders and instructions, just as she had as a child. She had not forgotten Mordecai's counsel, the ways of her people, the history of her race, or the commandments of God.

In the course of time, a murderous bully named Haman rose to power, becoming the prime minister. All the royal officials were ordered to kneel down and prostrate themselves before Haman. But whenever Haman passed by Mordecai at the king's gate, Esther's teacher would not bow or pay him honor. "Why do you disobey the king's command?" the king's officials asked Mordecai, day after day

(Est. 3:3). The faithful Jew refused to go along with a civil law that he believed opposed God's commandments, regardless of the consequences.

How could Mordecai have known what evil would come from Haman's hatred? If he had known, would he still have refused to render homage to Haman? There can be no doubt: Mordecai honored only one God. And for that privilege, he found himself willing to pay with the price of his own life.

Not surprisingly, Mordecai's firm refusal to revere Haman enraged the king's top aide. And the scope of Haman's hatred is revealed by his scheme to destroy not only Mordecai but every Jew in the empire. Every Jew!

Haman went to the king: "There is a certain people dispersed and scattered among the peoples in all the provinces of your kingdom whose customs are different from those of all the other people and who do not obey the king's laws; it is not in the king's best interest to tolerate them. If it pleases the king, let a decree be issued to destroy them, and I will put ten thousand talents [375 tons] of silver into the royal treasury for the men who carry out this business" (Est. 3:8–9).

In Haman's statement we hear the same Hitlerian hiss that will usher in the Holocaust some twenty-five centuries later: They are different ... their customs are not like ours ... it is not in our interest to tolerate them. Therefore, let a decree be issued commanding the king's men to kill them.

Let us destroy them all.

The king agreed, and when Mordecai heard about the coming annihilation of his people, he tore his clothes, put on sackcloth and ashes, and walked through Susa wailing loudly and bitterly. Jews across the empire entered into mourning with weeping and fasting.

Esther Advances

> *Guard my life and rescue me; let me not be put to shame,*
> *for I take refuge in you. May integrity and uprightness*
> *protect me, because my hope is in you.* Psalm 25:20–21

*E*sther heard about Mordecai's wailing from her servants. In great distress, she sent him new clothing, but he refused. So she dispatched Hathach, a trustworthy eunuch, to ask what was wrong.

To Hathach, Mordecai confided every detail of the prime minister's plan for the annihilation of the Jews across the empire. Tell Esther, he said, even providing an exact copy of the edict's text. Urge the queen "to go into the king's presence to beg for mercy and plead with him for her people." (Est. 4:8). The eunuch immediately understood the severity of Mordecai's request.

Hearing Hathach's report, Esther responded with a certain measure of self-protection and royal loyalty. Aware that any covert communication could be intercepted, she prudently prepared a legally accurate reply for Hathach to deliver to Mordecai:

> All the king's officials and the people of the royal provinces know that for any man or woman who approaches the king in the inner court without being summoned the king has but one law: that he be put to death. The only exception to this is for the king to extend the gold scepter to him and spare his life. But thirty days have passed since I was called to go to the king. (Esther 4:11)

On one hand, it was a reasonable response; on the other, the queen's self-protective reply might indicate she had not fully faced the fact that if she *didn't* risk execution, the king's edict would cause death for every Jew. Was Esther's odd reply a sign of spiritual strength — or shock-induced denial? Either way, Mordecai's words cut right to the heart of the matter when he once again appealed to the queen for help. Speaking as a father to his daughter, Israel's greatest advocate delivered the truth in no uncertain terms as he confronted his captive child's fear:

> Do not think that because you are in the king's house you alone of all the Jews will escape. For if you remain silent at this time, relief and deliverance for the Jews will arise from another place, but you and your father's family will perish. And who knows but that you have come to royal position for such a time as this? (Esther 4:13–14)

This time Esther did not flinch at Mordecai's words. *May this be the reason why I am living in this unholy place? Why God has allowed me to suffer this shame these past five years? May the God of Abraham be praised! Lord, may it be Your will to deliver my people!*

As if Esther had emerged from an extended hibernation, her mind snapped to attention and her heart went on full alert. After years of emotional numbness, she once again felt pain and hope, inspiration and anger. Esther's second response to Mordecai, so completely unlike the first, shows she was ready for action: "Go, gather together all the Jews who are in Susa, and fast for me. Do not eat or drink for three days, night or day. I and my maids will fast as you do. When this is done, I will go to the king, even though it is against the law. And if I perish, I perish" (Est. 4:16).

It was an extreme fast — no food *or* water for three days. As she faced the prospect of increasing physical weakness,

Esther turned her full attention to the Lord, her sure source of strength and the only hope for Israel's salvation.

A woman of courage, indeed.

The Queen's Restraint

*Redeem Israel, O God, from all
their troubles!* Psalm 25:22

After the three days of prayer and fasting, Esther put on her royal robes and entered the inner court of the palace. She surrendered her future to God and stood in front of the king, confident that she had been divinely appointed for this crucial purpose. To her delight, King Xerxes looked at her and smiled. As he extended his golden scepter toward his favorite wife, Esther herself smiled, approached, and touched its tip.

God above, I thank you for sparing my life, she said silently. *May it be Your will to grant me wisdom on behalf of your nation, Israel, that we may be delivered from the hands of our enemies.*

Then Esther heard the words that she and her people had been praying for: "What is it, Queen Esther? What is your request? Even up to half the kingdom, it will be given you" (Est. 5:3).

The pivotal moment had arrived — an unparalleled test of Esther's courage and character. Her reply reflects a regal dignity born from above, the culmination of all her upbringing and Mordecai's diligent instruction. Rather than blurting out her desperate problem in an unchecked torrent of confession and supplication, Esther, probably still not yet twenty years old, wisely invited the king and Haman to attend a dinner she would prepare for them that evening.

The king — and Haman — enjoyed the dinner. The queen knew her husband as only a favorite wife could. Esther understood that in spite of all his wealth and power, King Xerxes was fascinated by wine, women, and food. When Xerxes asked again about Esther's earlier petition, she requested the king's — and Haman's — company at another feast the following day.

That night when Haman went home, he bragged to his wife and friends about the special treatment he was receiving at the royal palace but complained that the disrespectful Mordecai was still at the gate. His wife and friends advised him to build gallows and hang Mordecai. What a great idea! Haman ordered the gallows built without delay.

Israel's Deliverance

> *To you, O Lord, I lift up my soul; in you I trust, O my God. Do not let me be put to shame, nor let my enemies triumph over me.* Psalm 25:1–2

That night, the king could not sleep. After tossing and turning, he asked a servant to read to him from the record of his reign, the book of chronicles. He heard the story of Mordecai's heroic role in uncovering the assassination conspiracy. What's been done to honor this man? the king asked. Nothing.

Ah, as Haman is building a gallows to hang Mordecai, the king is wondering how to honor him. . . .

It was the beginning of the end for Haman. Drinking wine with the king at the queen's dinner party later in the day, Haman heard King Xerxes say, "Queen Esther, what is your petition? It will be given you. What is your request? Even up to half the kingdom, it will be granted" (Est. 7:2).

On this, the third time the king had asked, Queen Esther provided the critical information:

> If I have found favor with you, O king, and if it pleases your majesty, grant me my life — this is my petition. And spare my people — this is my request. For I and my people have been sold for destruction and slaughter and annihilation. If we had been merely sold as male and female slaves, I would have kept quiet, because no such distress would justify disturbing the king. (Esther 7:3–4)

The king asked Esther who could have done such a thing. And Esther named Haman. Without delay, Haman was hanged in place of Mordecai, whom the king appointed as prime minister. Then King Xerxes gave Haman's entire estate to Queen Esther. In place of Haman's decree of death, the king issued a new irrevocable edict granting Jews throughout his kingdom the right to assemble and protect themselves.

Today the Jewish celebration of Purim remains an annual observance of God's sovereign deliverance of Israel, the "days of feasting and joy and giving presents of food to one another and gifts to the poor" first instituted by Mordecai nearly 2,500 years ago. May we always honor Queen Esther's courageous example, never forgetting the shameful lowliness of her position before Israel's day of triumph. By looking to God as her strength, Esther acquired a quiet, humble confidence that God used in and for the salvation of her people.

Rosa Parks's Story

❧

*I*t is not our judgment of the situation which can show us what is wise but only the truth of the Word of God," wrote theologian Dietrich Bonhoeffer, who resisted Hitler's Third Reich at the cost of his life.[5]

A firm belief in the Bible's teachings about the eternal value of each person before God prompted Rosa Parks, a forty-two-year-old woman living in Montgomery, Alabama, in 1955, to take a courageous, quiet, wise stand for what was right.

Rosa Parks's witness is a modern-day reminder of Queen Esther's story. Both powerfully teach us about God's loving concern with human suffering and world affairs. They also affirm the moral necessity of standing up for what is right when the government goes wrong.

"If a government puts itself above the norms of civil society, it can be disobeyed and challenged in view of the revealed will of God; if it otherwise requires what conscience disallows," asserted Carl Henry, "one should inform government and be ready to take the consequences."[6]

Rosa Parks, like Esther, was ready to "take the consequences." Her high-risk decision on behalf of her people proved to be a turning point in the history of her nation.

In 1955, in Montgomery, Alabama, the law required segregated public transportation. On a city bus, black people were legally not allowed to sit in the same row with white people, nor could they sit across the aisle from anyone who was white. Custom dictated that black people pay at the front door, exit the bus, reenter by the rear door, and find an appropriate seat.

As white people boarded a city-owned vehicle, any black people riding on the bus were obliged to move to the rear seats once the "white section" had filled. But in Montgomery black people, not white, comprised the majority of bus riders, making the bus segregation law an especially humiliating daily reminder of the community's widespread racial intolerance.

One Woman's Decision

He guides me in paths of righteousness
for his name's sake. Psalm 23:3

On a Thursday evening — December 1, 1955 — Rosa Parks, a middle-aged African American, was riding home on a public bus after a long day at work as a seamstress at the Montgomery Fair Department Store's tailor shop. Though she was tired, Rosa's appearance clearly reflected her dignified, quiet confidence. A small hat, neatly secured to the crown of her swept-up hair, was the perfect accessory to the attractive gray suit she had picked out to wear early that morning.

It was still early in the evening when Rosa boarded the bus for home. Following her usual routine, she paid her fare, found a vacant seat, and sat down. But on this particular day, Rosa found that she could no longer ignore the widespread wrong being done to her people. When J. P. Blake, the driver of Rosa's bus, ordered the black people who were sitting in the fifth row (the first row of the "colored" section and the row Rosa was sitting in) to move to the rear to make room for a white man who was left without a seat, at first no one moved.

"Y'all better make it light on yourselves and let me have those seats," Mr. Blake said, apparently aware of the fact that Montgomery's segregation laws were the subject of increasingly heated debates around the country.

"I knew someone had to take the first step. So I made up my mind not to move," Rosa explains. "Since I had always been a strong believer in God, I knew that He was with me, and only He could get me through the next step."[7]

When three people sitting near Rosa got up and moved to the back of the bus, the soft-spoken, neatly dressed seamstress chose not to follow. For the first time in her life, she remained in her seat.

"I do not remember being frightened," recalls Rosa. "But I sure did not believe I would 'make it light' on myself by standing up. Our mistreatment was just not right, and I was tired of it. The more we gave in, the worse they treated us. I kept thinking about my mother and my grandparents, and how strong they were. I knew there was a possibility of being mistreated, but an opportunity was being given to me to do what I asked of others."[8]

Rosa adds: "I felt the Lord would give me the strength to endure whatever I had to face. God did away with all my fear. It was time for someone to stand up — or in my case, sit down. I refused to move."[9]

When Mr. Blake asked Rosa if she intended to get up and move, the well-mannered Montgomery citizen calmly replied, "No, I am not."

The bus driver warned Rosa he would have to phone the police. "Go ahead," she answered with full understanding of the possible consequences. And before five minutes had passed, two law enforcement officers arrived on the scene.

Mr. Blake pointed to the fifth row, to the small, demure-looking woman sitting quietly in the middle of the bus. He explained Rosa's refusal to stand up when he informed her that her seat was needed for white passengers. When one of the policemen asked Rosa why she refused to stand up, she replied with her own question, asking, "Why do you all push us around?"

"The law is the law and you're under arrest," the officer answered brusquely. And with these words, the policeman took Rosa into custody as a lawbreaker.

"I did not get on the bus to get arrested. I got on the bus to go home," Rosa admits. "Getting arrested was one of the worst days of my life."[10]

A Stand Worth Taking

> *Even though I walk through a valley dark as death I fear no evil, for thou art with me, thy staff and thy crook are my comfort.* Psalm 23:4 NEB

At the moment she decided not to move to the back of the bus, Rosa Parks wasn't thinking about starting a civil rights movement in her community. "When I sat down on the bus the day I was arrested, I was thinking of going home," she explains. "I had made up my mind quickly about what it was that I had to do. I did not think of being physically tired or fearful. After so many years of oppression and being a victim of the mistreatment that my people had suffered, not giving up my seat — and whatever I had to face after not giving it up — was not important. I did not feel any fear at sitting in the seat I was sitting in. All I felt was tired."[11]

Rosa never considered that her private decision would become the much publicized turning point in her people's struggle for racial equality in America. How could she have possibly known that her quiet, confident decision to follow God's leading would result in a citywide bus boycott that would last for 381 days and capture the attention of the entire nation?

"I had no idea that history was being made," Rosa openly admits. "I was just tired of giving in. Somehow, I felt that what I did was right by standing up to that bus driver. I did not think about the consequences. I knew that I could have been lynched, manhandled, or beaten when the police came. I chose not to move."[12]

Thankfully, Rosa's mindful civil disobedience on the bus that night in Montgomery, Alabama, did not result in her being lynched, manhandled, or beaten by the police. Still, after her arrest, Rosa suffered the humiliation of being taken to the city jail, fingerprinted, and placed behind bars.

Once Rosa was locked in her jail cell, she reflected on what had happened that evening. The people she knew on the bus had remained quiet. No one had tried to defend her. No one had even called her husband to tell him what had happened. Feeling isolated and alone, the unlikely hero of the American civil rights movement prayed silently and waited for someone to come to her defense.

But she did not cry.

Answered Prayers

You prepare a table before me in the presence
of my enemies. You anoint my head with oil;
my cup overflows. Psalm 23:5

It is strange: after the arrest, I never did reach the breaking point of shedding tears," Rosa says, as if still
amazed by the unexplainable peace that comforted her
weary heart on that decisive December night.[13]

Like Esther, Rosa had never forgotten the vivid Old Testament stories she had heard while growing up. "From my
upbringing and the Bible, I learned people should stand up for
their rights, just as the children stood up to Pharaoh," she
explains. "Many people cannot relate to the feelings of frustration that we, as black people, felt in the 1950s. For many years
black people accepted the treatment.... It was a long time coming, but finally, as a group, we demanded, 'Let my people go.'"[14]

News of Rosa's arrest spread quickly among Montgomery's
civil rights supporters. Within hours of her arrest, three of
Rosa's friends—Clifford and Virginia Durr and Edgar D.
Nixon—arrived at the jail and swiftly made arrangements for
Rosa's immediate release. The Durrs were white; Clifford, an
attorney, and Virginia were actively involved in the desegrega-
tion movement. Edgar Nixon, a black man, was the president of
the Alabama chapter of the NAACP (National Association for
the Advancement of Colored People). Rosa was soon released
under the supervision of Edgar Nixon and the Durrs, with husband, Raymond, at her side.

Years later, looking back on that night in 1955, Rosa had
no regrets about her moral choice. She wrote in her book,
Quiet Dignity, "Human dignity must be respected at all times.

Not standing up that night on the bus was a matter of self-respect. Every day of my life, I have wanted to be treated with respect. I had expected and hoped that others would feel the same. But because of my race, I was denied that respect. In many ways, that still happens to us today. . . . I am concerned about any discrimination, of any people, regardless of race or other physical differences."[15]

Rosa Parks's arrest — and her carefully considered refusal to pay the fourteen-dollar fine imposed on her peaceful act of civil disobedience — proved the starting point for a history-making bus boycott that lasted for just over a year. The day after the Supreme Court's written order that declared Alabama's bus segregation laws unconstitutional was officially received in Montgomery, on December 20, 1956, black people once again rode the city's buses — and for the first time, they sat wherever space was available.

In time Rosa Parks's humble determination to peacefully resist hatred and intolerance would place her among the outstanding American women of the twentieth century. Though Rosa was tired at the end of a long day's work that fateful day in 1955, she would have been happy to give up her seat to someone who needed it more than she — to an elderly person or a mother with her infant child. But on that particular evening, physical fatigue was not the main reason Rosa Parks remained in her seat on that bus.

Though we're never told the reason why God is never mentioned by name in the book of Esther, we clearly see him everywhere throughout her story — accomplishing his sovereign will, teaching us to discern the difference between civil laws and divine commandments, revealing the end result of pride and prejudice, exalting the humble people who believed their destiny was determined by their God, not by an earthly king. In Rosa's story, the Lord's hand also is evident, reminding us:

To the faithful you show yourself faithful;
to those with integrity you show integrity.
To the pure you show yourself pure,
but to the wicked you show yourself hostile.
You rescue those who are humble,
but you humiliate the proud.
Lord, you have brought light to my life;
my God, you light up my darkness.
In your strength I can crush an army;
with my God I can scale a wall.

—Psalm 18:25–29 NLB

Where cross the crowded ways of life,
  Where sound the cries of race and clan
Above the noise of selfish strife,
  We hear Thy voice, O Son of Man.

In haunts of wretchedness and need,
  On shadowed thresholds dark with fears,
From paths where hide the lures of greed,
  We catch the vision of Thy tears.

From tender childhood's helplessness,
  From woman's grief, man's burdened toil,
From famished souls, from sorrow's stress,
  Thy heart has never known recoil.

The cup of water given for Thee
  Still holds the freshness of Thy grace;
Yet long the multitudes to see
  The sweet compassion of Thy face.

O Master, from the mountain side,
  Make haste to heal these hearts of pain;
Among these restless throngs abide,
  O tread the city's streets again.

Till sons of men shall learn Thy love,
  And follow where Thy feet have trod;
Till glorious from Thy heaven above,
  Shall come the City of our God.

— Frank Mason North, 1903

Conclusion

❧

*S*ometimes it's easy to start thinking in terms of the *if onlys*: If only I were more sensitive to the Holy Spirit, I would never be thoughtless, vain, or temperamental. If only I studied Scriptures more often, I would be able to triumphantly refute Satan's accusations without suffering from his attacks. If only I prayed more continuously, I would benefit from God's blessings to such an extent that I could feel joy in every life circumstance. If only I had more faith, I would not have so much back pain ... would not experience this kind of financial difficulty ... would not have lost my husband to cancer ... would not be the mother of a disabled child ... would not have been in that car accident last week.

But are these expectations very realistic given what it means to live and die in a fallen world? Of course not. And yet, when the Spirit's fruit — love, joy, peace, patience — seem slow to ripen or, at times, appear absent altogether, we may find ourselves discounting God's grace as we push ourselves harder and harder. We may try to prove to ourselves and others that we're worthy of the Lord's love. We may mistakenly think that the Spirit's fruit can be bartered for — earned in exchange for our good works and good behavior. Or we may simply opt to neglect our need to quietly consider God's great majesty every day as we willingly rest our hearts and minds in our gentle Shepherd's renewing presence.

Think of how much energy and effort it takes to try to become perfect according to one's own ideas of perfection, to maintain an image of one's self based on our own and other people's opinions. Remember, William Temple, the archbishop of Canterbury, said it simply led to anxiety — worrying over whether you'll always catch the ball. In the long run, it just doesn't work. Is this state of anxiety, stress, tension, and uneasiness what the Christian life is all about?

Isaac of Syria knew this about humility: "Blessed is the man who knows his own weakness, because awareness of this becomes for him the foundation and beginning of all that is good and beautiful. . . . But no one can perceive his own weakness unless he has been remiss a little, has neglected some small thing, has been surrounded by trials, either in the matter of things which cause the body suffering, or in that of ways in which the soul is subject to passions. Only then, by comparing his own weakness, will he realize how great is the assistance which comes from God."[16]

The Savior who invites us to rest and abide with him makes it possible for us to draw near to his holy presence by graciously covering our weakness and compassionately bearing our pain with and for us. But, like Esther and Rosa, we must choose: *Surrendering to the Lord's design for our lives requires our strenuous cooperation with the Holy Spirit's bondage-breaking, liberating, life-giving power.*

Looking up, asking God for help — that prayer of supplication itself humbles us. Isaac of Syria also noted that a heart that is not humbled will wander, but, conversely, "humility concentrates the heart."[17]

And looking to God leads us to the strength cited by the prophet Isaiah: "In quietness and in confidence shall be your strength" (Isa. 30:15 KJV). Esther and Rosa were not concerned about their own perfection or their own welfare, but saw themselves as one among many, stepping out in obedience to what they knew was just and right. They knew they weren't perfect. By their example, we see how humble confidence, rather than perfection, allowed God to use and work through them. And the same is true for us.

Points for Reflection

1. God's strength has been especially evident to me when my own weakness leads me to ...
2. As I thought about Esther's situation, I realized ...
3. Knowing the Lord is acquainted with every aspect of who I am — emotionally, physically, and spiritually — encourages me to let go of ...
4. Rosa Parks's story shows that even "ordinary" Christian women can do extraordinary things when we ...
5. Following Christ is both harder and easier than my own ideas about self-perfection because ...
6. God's Word helps me to grow in humble confidence when ...

Prayer: Here I am, Lord, counting on Your strength to be made perfect in weakness according to the richness of Your grace. I trust You to finish Your design for my life as You work within my mind and heart; I ask for humble confidence as You show me how to apply Your truth to all of life. Grant me quiet courage to live by Your Word. In Jesus' name, I pray. Amen.

Praise the Lord, O my soul;
  all my inmost being, praise his holy name.
Praise the Lord, O my soul,
  and forget not all his benefits —
who forgives all your sins
  and heals all your diseases,
who redeems your life from the pit
  and crowns you with love and compassion,
who satisfies your desires with good things
  so that your youth is renewed like the eagle's.

The Lord works righteousness
  and justice for all the oppressed.

He made known his ways to Moses,
  his deeds to the people of Israel:
The Lord is compassionate and gracious,
  slow to anger, abounding in love.
He will not always accuse,
  nor will he harbor his anger forever;
he does not treat us as our sins deserve
  or repay us according to our iniquities.
For as high as the heavens are above the earth,
  so great is his love for those who fear him;
as far as the east is from the west,
  so far has he removed our transgressions from us.

— Psalm 103:1–12

Life is a splendid gift. There is nothing small in it. For the greatest grow by God's law out of the smallest.[18]

— Florence Nightingale (1820–1910)

What is His will? — that I may go
  And do it in the hope
That light will rise and spread and grow.
  As deed enlarges scope.

I need not search the sacred book
  To find my duty clear;
Scarce in my bosom need I look,
  It lies so very near.

Henceforward I must watch the door
  Of word and action too;
There's one thing I must do no more,
  Another I must do.

Alas, these are such little things!
  No glory in their birth!
Doubt from their common aspect springs,
  If God will count them worth.

But here I am not left to choose,
  My duty is my lot;
And weighty things will glory lose,
  If small ones are forgot.

I am not worthy high things yet;
  I'll humbly do my own;
Good care of sheep may so beget
  A fitness for Thy throne.

Ah fool! Why dost thou reason thus?
  Ambition's very fool!
Through high and low, each glorious,
  Shines God's all-perfect rule.

'Tis God I need, not rank in good;
'Tis Life, not honor's meed;
With Him to fill my every mood,
I am content indeed.[19]

— George MacDonald (1824–1905)

Chapter Five

Through Vocation

*A story is told of Jesus and his disciples walking one day
along a stony road. Jesus asked each of them to choose a stone
to carry for him. John, it is said, chose a large one while Peter
chose the smallest. Jesus led them then to the top of a mountain and commanded that the stones be made bread. Each disciple, by this time tired and hungry, was allowed to eat the bread
he held in his hand, but of course Peter's was not sufficient to
satisfy his hunger. John gave him some of his.*

*Some time later Jesus again asked the disciples to pick up a
stone to carry. This time Peter chose the largest of all. Taking
them to a river, Jesus told them to cast the stones into the water.
They did so, but looked at one another in bewilderment.*

"For whom," asked Jesus, "did you carry the stone?"[1]

— Elisabeth Elliot

The cookie press sat on the counter next to three non-
stick aluminum baking sheets, each freshly washed
and waiting to be used to help turn out five dozen sugar
cookies for our Christmas Eve buffet. As I blended the
ingredients together — unsalted butter, an egg, granulated

sugar, a little salt, enriched flour, and an ample splash of almond extract — I started thinking about which designs would work best.

I loaded the cookie press with the sticky pale yellow dough and then sorted through about a dozen templates and selected several patterns: stars, trees, wreaths, and ribbons. For one cookie, then another, and another, I squeezed the trigger to force the dough from the press, repeating the same shape until I was ready to switch to a new design. My son helped me sprinkle yellow sugar crystals on the stars, red on the ribbons, and green on the trees and wreaths. When the cookies were decorated, we popped the pans into the oven and awaited the results.

Less than an hour later, our efforts had produced several baskets of delicately browned, tastefully decorated, mouth-watering Christmas cookies, soon to be enjoyed with spiced cider, eggnog, fruitcake, English trifle, and other traditional treats of the season, calories and fat grams notwithstanding.

Compare this to another type of shaping and baking done not in the family kitchen, but in a ceramic studio. Prepared from scratch, the clay used in making pottery must be mixed in large tubs (preferably sturdy plastic garbage containers), kneaded on a table to remove air bubbles, and then cured. It's a tedious, muddy, time-consuming job — which is why many people prefer to buy their clay and glazes ready-made. But the most dedicated craftsperson walks through each step, from mixing clay to combining chemicals for glazes; this allows for greater mastery over her materials and enables the potter to create original pieces that can't be duplicated.

If the pottery is to be hand thrown, the potter uses a kick wheel to turn the clay. Her strong, determined hands shape the whirling clay purposefully, patiently, to produce a piece of uniform density with a symmetrical appearance. It requires skill to make pottery that can withstand the firing process. Even slight imperfections can cause the piece of clay to explode, crack, or fall apart when baked.

When shaped on a kick wheel instead of in a mold, the ball of soft clay, as it responds to the potter's hands, becomes a one-of-a-kind item. Each piece bears the imprint of its creator's personality and talent, a work of art representing the cumulative knowledge the artisan applied to its construction.

The results can be pleasantly surprising or frustratingly disappointing. Pottery-making is never a predictable process: it is a gradual, step-by-step interaction between the artisan and her specially selected natural materials; to obtain the desired outcome, the process requires patience, planning, and skill.

Think back over your life. Do you remember times when you felt more like a pressed-out Christmas cookie than a handcrafted masterwork? I admit, sometimes the one-size-for-all life seems easier, less complicated, and more predictable. Sometimes we like to fit into someone else's notion of who we should be.

Even within the church there can be pressure placed on women to adopt a photocopy mentality concerning discipleship, suggesting that we duplicate an ideal that may not be based on biblical norms. But historically — as you've seen in previous chapters — Christ's calling and the work of his Spirit have never meant that one person needs to be just like everybody else.

Yielding to the slow but steady process through which God shapes and transforms us into the image of the divine Master requires our remaining on the Potter's wheel — a steady refusal to slip off into a self-manufactured mold that offers a quick fit with the rest of the crowd, a firm trust in the final outcome of our Maker's promised handiwork.

"A holy life is not an ascetic, or gloomy, or solitary life, but a life regulated by divine truth and faithful in Christian duty," asserted Tryon Edwards. "It is living above the world while we are still in it."[2] When we look at women of the Bible — Hannah, Mary, Jesus' mother, the Samaritan woman who became an evangelist, and Mary of Magdala, for example — we catch glimpses of women living in the world and still managing with God's help to set their hearts and minds "on things above, not on earthly things" (Col. 3:1). Throughout the history of Christianity, we see women transformed by their Creator's artistry, women with vital work to do, women called to play an active role in serving Christ. These women willingly yielded to God's shaping process. Rather than conforming to a comfortable cultural template, they placed themselves in the Master's hands.

"Get to know the God of your ancestors. Worship and serve him with your whole heart and with a willing mind," wrote the prophet Ezra, the presumed author of the Old Testament Chronicles. "For the Lord sees every heart and understands and knows every plan and thought. If you seek him, you will find him" (1 Chron. 28:9 NLB).

If you seek him you will find him. Certainly Priscilla, the apostle Paul's coworker, understood this vital truth as she lovingly lived her life for Jesus Christ, as did Hilda of Whitby, an incredible seventh-century woman whose influence helped bring Britain out of the Dark Ages. These are stories worth remembering when we ponder the question: *Lord, what is the work You are calling me to do in Your name today?*

Priscilla's Story

As we peer back through time to the earliest Christians, we may sometimes wonder what was it like to be a woman uniquely called by God in the first years of the church — an era when being a Christian in itself was dangerous, when Roman emperors issued edicts forbidding religious freedom and executed unwavering Christian converts.

Time, distance, and cultural differences prevent us from obtaining an exact picture of the courageous people and historic events that shaped the first churches in Rome, Corinth, Ephesus, and elsewhere. We have no eyewitness news agencies to bring us live video feeds, no network reporters carrying constant radio commentary from the birthplaces of the church to anyone tuning in to listen.

Yet the essential facts have survived. We still can be encouraged by our faith's predecessors. Though the images are often intriguingly obscure, the brief glimpses we get of our heroines in the faith are solid and real, full of hope, truth, triumph, and inspiration.

Among the valiant women we meet in the New Testament, one clearly catches our attention — Priscilla who, with her husband, Aquila, and the apostle Paul, did not shirk from her providentially appointed role in sharing the Gospel with Jews and Gentiles alike. In Priscilla's story I see the luminous outline of grace, commitment, and devotion.

Priscilla was born and raised a Jew, just as her Master had been, most likely in a devout home where Sabbath celebrations called for women's creative involvement in ceremonial rituals and blessings, in a city where the religious persecution of her people substantially predated Christ's execution. Courageous faith was not unfamiliar to her.

Serving the one true God in a hostile society dedicated to Roman deities prepared Priscilla's heart early in life for the work her Lord called her to do in adulthood. When we first read of Priscilla and Aquila, we're told they are recently displaced political refugees, forced to move out of Rome by an edict issued by the Emperor Claudius. This edict was made around A.D. 50.

The whole Jewish community was disbanded, displaced, torn from their homes. I can hardly imagine those painful decisions: *Where shall we go? How much can we take? What must we leave? Will we ever be allowed to come back?*

Aquila had not been born in Rome but in Pontus, a region in Asia Minor, east of Greece. Priscilla's national origin is never made clear. Was she a Roman citizen? Where and when did she meet her husband? We don't know. But since these two are always named together, as a couple, we can assume they were closely associated with one another not only through marriage but through their work and ministry. That Priscilla's name is usually mentioned before Aquila's — an exceptional practice in those days — indicates she may have held a higher social rank than her husband. Or it may be that Paul and Luke (writing the Acts of the Apostles) sought to specifically honor Priscilla's church-related achievements by naming her first.

Few women in Priscilla's day were officially active in public life. They could not vote; did not serve in government as senators, magistrates, or judges; and were not priests. This did not mean, however, that women did not directly shape society or the early church. On the contrary, within the privacy of their homes, women could — and did — have a vital influence on shaping every aspect of community life.

A review of the few short passages in which Priscilla appears (Acts 18:1–4, 18–21, 24–26; Rom. 16:3–5; 1 Cor. 16:19; and 2 Tim. 4:19) can provoke us to ask: Exactly when did Priscilla and Aquila become Christians? Was her Jewish upbringing instrumental in fostering her deep understanding of the Messiah's coming? Did they have children? Though we can only guess at the answers, we gain a deeper appreciation for her important role in the early church by taking a closer look at her life and story.

A Starting Place

> *For he has rescued us from the dominion of darkness and brought us into the kingdom of the Son he loves, in whom we have redemption, the forgiveness of sins.* Colossians 1:13–14

Both Priscilla and Aquila were "tentmakers" — a term applied generally to all leatherworkers. It is easy to picture Priscilla's hands as she sat on a bench, working side by side with Aquila, cutting and sewing the thick, tanned skins of goats, sheep, and cattle. The trade demanded a precise form of strength from her callused and sinewy fingers. Experience guided every able movement, each efficient touch. Not a single moment or a leftover scrap of material was wasted.

While their hands steadily threaded the hides, their voices mingled conversation of lost dreams, future hopes, present realities.

We can imagine Priscilla sharing her concerns with her husband as she sat next to him in their shop: "Sometimes I think about how nice it would be to relocate somewhere permanently, knowing we could live in one place for the remainder of our lives," she might have told Aquila on a particularly lonely day.

Then perhaps Priscilla added: "Tell me again about the place where you grew up, what your family was like. I like to picture them in my mind as we work. It's so difficult not living near our families, not being able to settle down near them. But I feel very close to your loved ones, Aquila, whenever you share your favorite stories about them with me. I still haven't grown tired of hearing them."

Maybe they were heading back to Aquila's birthplace when they got off the boat and settled for a while in Corinth, Greece. Corinth had become the economic hub of Greece, a thriving port city. There was a large Jewish community there, tradespeople trying to give one another some support.

Priscilla and Aquila probably lived in an area crowded with people practicing the tentmaking craft, eventually becoming members of an artisan trade guild. Their practical leatherwork vocation allowed Priscilla and Aquila to spend their days together, in a home-based shop.

Priscilla knew how fortunate they were — being a team, being self-employed craftsmen, neither peasants nor encumbered with wealth. They could set their own hours. Even, as they'd learned, pick up and move to a new city on short notice with some assurance that their services would be needed in any location.

They hadn't been in Corinth long when the apostle Paul arrived at their home for an extended visit. Because he was also a tentmaker, he stayed and worked with Aquila and Priscilla, and on each Sabbath, he went to the synagogue and persuasively reasoned with Jews and Greeks alike. It's possible that this is where Priscilla and her husband were converted to Christ as they listened to Paul's divinely inspired preaching. Or perhaps they were already Christians when Paul showed up at their door in Corinth. In any case, Paul had specifically searched for Priscilla and Aquila — and he clearly felt at home with this unique couple.

It seems Paul stayed in Corinth for eighteen months, teaching in the synagogue, working in his friends' home shop, talking as he sewed, laughing at Priscilla's table, listening to her insights.

Elton Trueblood points to Paul's words as a clear indication of the kind of fellowship these dear saints enjoyed together as they learned to "teach and admonish one another with all wisdom" (Col. 3:16). "The most reasonable picture which these words suggest," says Dr. Trueblood, "is that of a group of modest Christians sitting in a circle in some simple room, sharing with one another their hopes, their failures, and their prayers. The key words are 'one another.' There are no mere observers or auditors; *all are involved.*"[3]

Can you imagine the rich dialogues and powerful prayers that must have proceeded from the long hours Paul spent with Priscilla and Aquila? What must it have been like to have so much uninterrupted time with this inspired — and inspiring — apostle? To hear God's Word coming forth from the man who would later write most of the Bible's epistles?

Speaking of Priscilla and Aquila, Gien Karssen notes, "Paul well knew that the best kind of training he could give came from being together day after day.... Each day Paul tailored the Word of God to their needs. And they learned how to apply it."[4] He grew to love and appreciate this family — their physical work and also their spiritual conviction and vocation — with whom he had so much in common.

Without question, Priscilla's vocation benefited from her willingness to take significant personal risks, to challenge prescribed life patterns. She was personally tutored in her faith by Paul. She was educated, well-traveled, and skilled in her trade. Above all, she was generous, compassionate, and brave — a woman who chose to open her home to others, sharing food, fellowship, teaching, and worship with them in Jesus' name.

Life at Priscilla's House

> *We proclaim him, admonishing and teaching everyone with all wisdom, so that we may present everyone perfect in Christ.* Colossians 1:28

Throughout her life, working at home offered Priscilla a considerable advantage, where meals became an extension of her art, prayer meetings an extension of her meals, study of the Scriptures an extension of her prayer meetings, and teaching an extension of her study of the Scriptures. I say amen to Jo Berry's assessment of Priscilla: "She viewed her entire life as a ministry dedicated to her Lord Jesus Christ. Everything she did, whether as homemaker, wife, teacher, or friend, was an outcropping of her Christianity. Christ was her primary focus, her first love, the prominent, abiding center of her existence."[5]

Priscilla's life was characterized by a continuous blending of her work, home, worship, beliefs, and relationships. Faith and craftsmanship merged with her marriage and ministry. Her focus remained on the tasks at hand, the guests at her table, the worship of her community, and the life-changing Gospel of Christ.

From the brief snapshots of Priscilla that Paul gave us, we see the integral role she played not only in his life but in the lives of those privileged to be guided by her godly wisdom in critical times at the founding of the Christian church. And all of this proceeded from Priscilla's life as Christ's disciple as she lived, worked, ate, worshiped, and taught in her home.

After eighteen months in Corinth, Paul packed his bags to leave town. Perhaps as a result of religious persecution after Paul was taken to court by orthodox members of the synagogue where he had often preached, Priscilla and Aquila left with him and sailed east toward Syria and the city of Ephesus, the capital of Rome's Asian province. Upon reaching Ephesus, Priscilla and Aquila decided to stay. Paul continued on, traveling from city to city.

Once again, Priscilla found herself setting up a business, making a home, reaching out to her new community — a community made up of unfamiliar cultural routines and countless strangers. Before long, another articulate rabbi arrived on the scene: Apollos, a gifted orator from the city of Alexandria. Like Paul, he spoke in the synagogue, but with a notable difference: Though Apollos "knew about Jesus," Priscilla and Aquila identified inconsistencies in his understanding of the Gospel and privately offered him their assistance. Though Luke does not explain Priscilla's role in Apollos's training, she and Aquila "invited him to their home and explained to him the way of God more adequately" (Acts 18:26). Priscilla's home-based vocation had officially expanded to include teaching. When Apollos wanted to leave to preach in Corinth, it's likely that Priscilla and Aquila gave him their blessing and may have composed the letter that encouraged the Corinthian disciples to welcome Apollos.

Later, when the news about Apollos's helpfulness and powerful religious debates in Corinth reached Priscilla and Aquila, I can picture them celebrating God's excellent plan for building Christ's church with plenty of hugs, spontaneous laughter, and a Spirit-filled prayer of thanksgiving.

A Church — and a Saint — in the Making

> *My purpose is that they may be encouraged in heart and united in love, so that they may have the full riches of complete understanding, in order that they may know the mystery of God, namely, Christ, in whom are hidden all the treasures of wisdom and knowledge.* Colossians 2:2–3

Not long after Apollos left for Corinth, Paul returned to Ephesus, where once again he worked in Priscilla's and Aquila's leathershop. The visit was brief, just three months, terminated by Paul's permanent banishment from the Ephesian synagogue. With Apollos's and Paul's departures, Priscilla's life certainly became less tumultuous for a few years, thereby allowing her work and ministry to touch many people's lives with the matchless love of Jesus Christ. She must have stayed busy day and night as she tended to the needs of her family, household, business, and the flourishing church that met in her home.

Priscilla, Virginia Stem Owens points out, "saw her life as a whole cloth. She allowed neither the products nor the small factory she operated to dominate her life. Thus when opportunity arose for her to teach, to counsel, to organize, she was open to those vocations as well. For her, making a living served the larger task of making a life. And because she maintained this larger vision, her work was more than profitable — it was priceless."[6]

Priscilla and Aquila eventually moved back to Rome after Claudius died. In his letter to the believers in Rome, Paul sends greetings to the couple, calling them "my fellow workers in Christ Jesus" who "risked their lives" for him (Rom. 16:3–4). Obviously they again had established a church, for Paul sends greetings to "the church that meets at their house" (v. 5).

Wherever she lived, Priscilla's domicile proved to be a prototype. In cities where trade guilds adopted patron deities, citizens regularly ate sacrificial food at community banquets, and religious factions violently struggled for political power, Christians sought and found vital refuge in the shelter of one another's households. As the body of Christ grew, private homes — not specially designed temples, synagogues, cathedrals, or other familiar forms of religious buildings — were the primary place of worship for the first three hundred years of the Christian church.

Tradition tells us that Priscilla and Aquila were martyred for their faith — a final act of courage for a founding mother of the church of Christ — a woman who followed the one true God wherever he chose to lead her.

Hilda of Whitby's Story

To get to the story of Hilda, one of Britain's most note-worthy canonized saints, let's fill in a bit of history, starting with an ancestor who was a missionary in her own right: France's Princess Bertha, daughter of the king of Paris.

Toward the end of the sixth century, Bertha consented to move to England — to marry the pagan King Ethelbert of Kent — if, and only if, she were allowed to bring with her a devout priest, Liudhard. When Bertha arrived in England, she was happy to find a few Christian churches still standing — remnants of the Roman occupation. She and Liudhard established worship in one of those tiny churches, in Canterbury. As queen she restored the building, which today is considered the oldest church structure in England.

As with many kings who married Christians, Ethelbert was not quickly convinced of Christ's true lordship. Many of his subjects converted to Christianity before he did. But four years after the pope sent an emissary to England, the king of Kent became a Christian. Without a doubt, Ethelbert's conversion was influenced by his wife and this emissary, who became the first archbishop of Canterbury. It was a decisive turning point for the growth of Christian faith in Kent and, later, all of England.

A Christian Lineage

> *So then, just as you received Christ Jesus as Lord, con-*
> *tinue to live in him, rooted and built up in him, strength-*
> *ened in the faith as you were taught, and overflowing with*
> *thankfulness.* Colossians 2:6–7

Bertha and Ethelbert had a daughter, Princess Ethelberga, who in her mother's care grew in faith. When
another British king, Edwin of York, asked to marry Ethelberga, Ethelbert and Bertha said no, "it was not permissible
for a Christian maiden to be given in marriage to a heathen
husband, lest the Christian faith and sacraments be profaned
by her association with a King who was wholly ignorant of
the worship of the true God."[7] Nevertheless, a marriage
agreement was made, with two stipulations: first, that Ethelberga and her followers would be free to worship according
to their faith; and second, that the king would adopt the faith
himself if, after seriously considering Christianity, he considered it more satisfactory and sacred than his own religion.

So Ethelberga married Edwin with the hope that he
would be saved by the steady example of his believing wife.
Like her mother, Ethelberga took a learned chaplain with
her to York as her spiritual counselor — the priest Paulinus.

Like his father-in-law, Edwin did not convert quickly.
But when he did, thousands of his subjects also converted,
including many members of his household. Among these
new believers was Edwin's nephew's daughter, a studious,
sober-minded girl named Hilda. While Hilda was very
young, her father was murdered by political enemies. Flee-
ing the country, her mother left Hilda with King Edwin and
Queen Ethelberga, who raised her as their own. On Easter
eve, 627, Hilda and King Edwin were baptized. Hilda being

thirteen, she was old enough to understand the importance of the sacrament.

Only six years later, Edwin was killed in a battle against the pagan king of Mercia. With the king's untimely death, Ethelberga fled back to her father's kingdom, taking along her own children, Hilda, and her faithful priest.

Because two princesses, a mother and her daughter, had refused to abandon their faith when required to marry pagan monarchs, two kings were converted through the examples of their believing wives. Countless Anglo-Saxons were introduced to Christ. And an exceptional woman named Hilda was providentially prepared to respond to God's call.

Hilda's Calling: To Serve God Alone

> *See to it that no one takes you captive through hollow and deceptive philosophy, which depends on human tradition and the basic principles of this world rather than Christ.*
> Colossians 2:8

*U*ntil the age of thirty-three, Hilda faithfully served as a renowned leader's descendant in the secular sphere of her society. As a noblewoman, she studied Latin, Greek, French, geography, mathematics, and other academic subjects while male counterparts were kept busy fighting barbarian invaders. Then a new calling came, and for the second half of her life, Hilda served Christ's church as an outstanding scholar and spiritual mentor.

Jonathan Edwards, the distinguished eighteenth-century preacher and president of Princeton University, noted: "The importance of religion is so great that no halfhearted exercise will suffice. In nothing is the state of our heart so crucial as in religion, and in nothing is lukewarmness so odious."[8] In 647 Hilda entered a convent in France, taking religious vows that symbolized her wholehearted devotion to Christ.

Shortly after she had chosen to quietly embrace this rigorous vocation, Hilda was summoned back to England by a bishop. He gave her a small plot of land on the north bank of the Wear River and a special assignment: She was to establish and administrate a small convent.

A year later, the bishop called her again. He had another job for her to do. He asked her to take charge of a monastery — for nuns *and* monks — in the village of Hartlepool. The men and women in the monastic community lived apart in adjacent quarters, complemented one another's study and work, supported each other in prayer, and worshiped together daily.

In the early English church, double monasteries were commonly under the direction of an abbess. "The abbess was not only a ruler, but also an educator at some of these 'coed' monasteries," according to professors Ruth Tucker and Walter Liefeld. "All things considered, monasticism had a great deal to offer women and continued to appeal to those who gladly renounced marriage for the privilege of devoting their lives in service to God."[9]

A Continuing Legacy

Since, then, you have been raised with Christ, set your
hearts on things above, where Christ is seated at the right
hand of God. Colossians 3:1

At Hartlepool, Hilda proved a wise, capable, and even-handed abbess — for nine years.

After her appointment, the scholarly abbess was greatly encouraged by the bishop to employ her considerable talents for the good of Christ's church in pagan England. By example, Hilda steadfastly promoted a high standard of learning and commitment to Christ. She personally demonstrated "the observance of justice, devotion, purity, and other virtues, but especially peace and charity," according to St. Bede, who noted that in Hilda's household "no one was rich or poor, for everything was held in common, and none possessed any personal property. So great was her prudence that not only ordinary folk, but kings and princes used to come and ask her advice in their difficulties. Those under her direction were required to make a thorough study of the Scriptures and occupy themselves in good works, in order that many might be found fitted for Holy Orders and the service of God's altar."[10]

Among those who sought Hilda's counsel was King Oswy, Edwin's sanctioned successor. As Oswy prepared to face the Pendians in battle, he made a promise to God: If the Lord saw fit to grant the king's army victory, Oswy would immediately donate land to the church, provide the means to establish a prestigious abbey, and send his daughter to live there.

Once his enemies had been soundly defeated, King Oswy kept his vow, placing his one-year-old daughter,

Aelfleda, in Hilda's care. At the meeting in Hartlepool, he gave a substantial plot of land to the abbess. The site, on the rugged coast of York, was called Streaneshalch, meaning "light of the beacon." He provided resources for Hilda to establish an abbey there, where Aelfleda would be raised as a daughter of Christ.

A Passion for Knowing Christ and Making Him Known

> *Therefore, as God's chosen people, holy and dearly loved, clothe yourselves with compassion, kindness, humility, gentleness, and patience. Bear with each other and forgive whatever grievances you may have against one another. Forgive as the Lord forgave you. And over all these virtues put on love, which binds them all together in perfect unity.* Colossians 3:12–14

In 657, Hilda officially opened a monastery at Streaneshalch, which came to be known as Whitby Abbey. With its great library, clear sense of academic purpose, solid commitment to prayer, and ongoing involvement in good works, the monastery for men and women, modeled after her house at Hartlepool, rapidly distinguished itself as a serious learning institution and spiritual training center.

The brothers and sisters in Hilda's community painstakingly illuminated manuscripts. They read and copied books by hand long before the invention of the printing press, solved complex mathematical puzzles, developed intricate choral harmonies in their worship of God, and looked after the spiritual and physical needs of all who lived in the area governed by the monastery. And these devout men and women did all of this and much more during the feudal Dark Ages, before Christianity was widely accepted in Britain.

No less than five bishops — Bishop Wilfrid II of York; Bishop John of Beverly; Archbishop Bosa of York; Bishop Ottfor of Worcester; Bishop Aetta of Colchester — came from Whitby, which served as a model for many colleges and universities.

In addition to this far-reaching legacy, Hilda is credited with yet another — playing a foundational role in the development of English literature. Not that she set out to do anything noteworthy. She simply listened carefully to a story floating around the grounds, that one of the local shepherds was singing an unusual song. Curious, she asked to see him and asked him to sing for her. He spoke only the common language, Anglo-Saxon, and in his own uneducated manner, he sang a long ballad about the story of Creation.

When she asked where he'd learned the song, he claimed he'd heard a voice telling him to sing the story of the world's birth. Hilda sensed that the Holy Spirit had inspired the song, as the man, named Caedmon, had never been taught about the Bible.

By the time Hilda was through with Caedmon, he was a monk at Whitby. She encouraged him to develop his unique song-writing talent, and he eventually wrote many Scripture-based songs in the vernacular Anglo-Saxon language — the first Bible stories really assimilated by the British peasants who did not know Latin. For her patronage and biblical instruction of this balladeer, some cite Hilda as influencing the development of English literature. (Make way for Beowulf!)

A Good and Faithful Servant

> *Let the word of Christ dwell in you richly as you teach and admonish one another with all wisdom, and as you sing psalms, hymns, and spiritual songs with gratitude in your hearts to God. And whatever you do, whether in word or deed, do it all in the name of the Lord Jesus, giving thanks to God the Father through him.* Colossians 3:16–17

Hilda's insistence on the comprehensive study of Holy Scripture and careful preparation for Christian service among all the members of her monastic household helped harvest good spiritual fruit for Britain, bringing spiritual nourishment to many people beyond the walls of her monastery. Her serenity in times of spiritual darkness and national peril must have been a balm indeed.

As one of England's most outstanding English abbesses, Hilda served at Whitby for more than twenty years, her passion for God being the driving force in her life.

In the last six years of her life, Hilda suffered a painful chronic illness. A devoted servant-leader until her death, she refused to cut back on her workload and continued her duties until she died quietly at Whitby Abbey on November 17, 680. Hilda's last message to her community was one of kindly encouragement "to keep the Gospel peace among yourselves and with others"; even at the end she reiterated the theme of Christian unity that had so often been the focus of her work and prayers.[11]

After Hilda's death, King Oswy's daughter, Aelfleda, became co-abbess with her mother, Eanfleda. A new generation of women led the renowned religious center where five eminent bishops, canonized saints, and Caedmon, the shepherd-poet of English literature, had been nurtured in their faith. Following in the footsteps of her spiritual mother and wise mentor, Aelfleda became widely known as a church mediator — the "comforter and best counselor of the whole province."[12]

Savior, Thy dying love
Thou gavest me,
Nor should I aught withhold,
Dear Lord, from Thee:
In love my soul would bow,
My heart fulfill its vow,
Some off-ring bring Thee now,
Something for Thee.

At the blest mercy seat,
Pleading for me,
My feeble faith looks up,
Jesus, to thee:
Help me the cross to bear,
Thy wondrous love declare,
Some song to raise, or pray'r,
Something for Thee.

Give me a faithful heart,
Likeness to Thee,
That each departing day
Henceforth may see
Some work of love begun,
Some deed of kindness done,
Some wand'rer sought and won,
Something for Thee.

All that I am and have,
Thy gifts so free,
In joy, in grief, thro' life,
Dear Lord, for Thee!
And when Thy face I see,
My ransomed soul shall be,
Thro' all eternity,
Something for Thee.

—Sylvanus Dryden Phelps (1816–1895)

Conclusion

Priscilla and Hilda had much in common. In whatever city God placed them, they picked up and continued their work and ministry. Hilda's spiritual gifts — knowledge, discernment, teaching, and hospitality — are reminiscent of Priscilla's. We honor these two women today not only for loving and serving the Lord with their whole hearts and minds, but for the manner in which they courageously went about doing God's business, in God's way.

The message is clear: "For we are God's workmanship, created in Christ Jesus to do good works which God prepared in advance for us to do" (Eph. 2:10). By faith we receive God's free gift of salvation; by grace we give our lives back to him as an expression of our love for his Son. Discovering our true vocation involves both the Lord's work within us and our willingness to accept our calling. Like Priscilla and Hilda, we have been uniquely fitted by our Creator with precisely the talents and abilities we need to fulfill God's plans for our lives.

And remember, it is a *unique* plan. In 1 Corinthians 3:6 Paul referred to Apollos, the Jewish man who had become a Christian under the tutelage of Priscilla and Aquila. Apollos eventually became a leader in the Corinthian church. Living in Ephesus, Paul had heard that the Corinthians were quarreling, some claiming to be followers of Paul, others followers of Apollos. Paul didn't want to hear this. He wrote:

What, after all, is Apollos? And what is Paul? Only servants, through whom you came to believe — as the Lord has assigned to each his task. I planted the seed, Apollos watered it, but God made it grow. So neither he who plants nor he who waters is anything, but only God, who makes things grow. The man who plants and the man who waters have one purpose, and each will be rewarded according to his own labor. For we are God's fellow workers. . . .

By the grace God has given me, I laid a foundation as an expert builder, and someone else is building on it. But each one should be careful how he builds. For no one can lay any foundation other than the one already laid, which is Jesus Christ. (1 Corinthians 3:5–11)

What does this passage say to me? That God gives us different jobs to do — whether planting or watering, witnessing or discipling. And in God's scheme, one job is not "more worthy" than another. Planting is just as important as watering — when we realize that it is God who works through our faithful service. In the kingdom of God the focus is on the Lord himself, not on the work we do on his behalf. Our service in the Kingdom is merely the joyful, singleminded, freely chosen response to Christ's call.

No matter what our vocation, we are to see ourselves as servants of our Lord, who graces us and assigns us tasks that he equips us to carry through on. The nineteenth-century Episcopal bishop Phillips Brooks said, "Do not pray for tasks equal to your powers. Pray for powers equal to your tasks."[13]

After we're born again, we begin working for a new boss. Whereas our previous employer used heavy-handed practices to keep us on his payroll, Jesus presents us with the promise that he will lighten our weighty loads by working right along with us. *Our Lord's management style perfectly fits who God created us to be.* When we voluntarily labor in his kingdom, following his guidance and direction, we receive what we need to become the Lord's active and vibrant servants.

I think we sometimes grow agitated that we aren't sure we've found "God's will" for our lives or our livelihood. We can learn a lesson from Priscilla and Hilda. I don't sense they fussed over the long-range plan. I think that in faith they always took the next step as God revealed it to them.

> *There's great truth in this old poem:*
> *From an old English parsonage, down by the sea*
> *There came in the twilight a message to me;*
> *Its quaint Saxon legend, deeply engraven,*
> *Hath, as it seems to me, teaching from Heaven.*
> *And on through the hours the quiet words ring*
> *Like a low inspiration — "DO THE NEXT THING."*[14]
>
> — Author Unknown

Stay in the Word. Pray for discernment and, as the wise Solomon advised, "Whatever your hand finds to do, do it with all your might" (Eccl. 9:10).

Points for Reflection

1. I believe the Lord is calling me to serve him today by . . .
2. Because my identity is based on who I am in Christ rather than on what I do, my vocation can never be a substitute for . . .
3. Priscilla's spiritual gifts were put to excellent use when she . . .
4. At this point in my life, I become less certain about God's calling when I . . .
5. As I read Hilda's story, I was most impressed by her influence upon . . .
6. I could better invest and use my personal resources — talents, finances, time, energy, education, spiritual gifts — if . . .

Prayer: Lord, help me to remember that I am here just for a few moments, a pilgrim heading toward Home. Thank You for creating me in Christ with appointed work to do. Please remind me of Your presence as I labor: I deeply desire to know that You are working here with me — my strength, my confidence, my life, my friend, and my Lord. Help me to clearly hear Your calling; give me the courage to follow where You lead me; teach me to use my time here wisely, for Your honor and glory. In Jesus' name, I pray. Amen.

One thing I ask of the Lord,
  one thing I seek:
that I may be constant in the house of the Lord
  all the days of my life,
to gaze upon the beauty of the Lord
  and to seek him in his temple.
For he will keep me safe under his roof
  in the day of misfortune;
he will hide me under the cover of his tent;
  he will raise me beyond reach of distress.
Now I can raise my head high
  above the enemy all about me;
so I will acclaim him with sacrifice before his tent
  and sing a psalm of praise to the Lord.

— Psalm 27:4–6 NEB

If God has called you, do not look over your shoulder
to see who is following you.[15]

— Corrie ten Boom (1892–1983)

I would be true, for there are those who trust me;
I would be pure, for there are those who care;
I would be strong, for there is much to suffer;
I would be brave, for there is much to dare;
I would be brave, for there is much to dare.

I would be friend of all — the foe, the friendless;
I would be giving, and forget the gift;
I would be humble, for I know my weakness;
I would look up, and laugh, and love, and lift;
I would look up, and laugh, and love, and lift.

I would be prayerful through each busy moment;
I would be constantly in touch with God;
I would be tuned to hear His slightest whisper;
I would have faith to keep the path Christ trod;
I would have faith to keep the path Christ trod.

— Howard A. Walter (1883–1918)

Chapter Six

✿

Give us clear vision that we may know where to stand and what to stand for, because unless we stand for something, we shall fall for anything.[1]

— Peter Marshall (1903–1949)

Have you ever experienced the challenge of keeping your love for the Lord clearly in focus? Do you find yourself being tempted to succumb to the "me first" ethic in your workplace, your neighborhood, your church, or your family? If so, you're certainly not alone.

We frequently feel pulled in a dozen different directions, pressured by contemporary role models who encourage us to look at a job or our looks as the central core of our identity — when our greatest joy and highest privilege as believers is designed to come from knowing, serving, and loving our Lord.

As Christ's followers, we don't have to wait for the perfect moment to surrender ourselves to God; the time to do it is right now, right where we are with whatever we already have.

We can follow the encouraging examples of women in the Word who shared their gifts, talents, and resources with the Lord. Like them, we are called to creatively express our womanhood as we work in God's great kingdom. The life pattern our Father lovingly cuts out for each of his daughters isn't "one size fits all": it's one of a kind — a never-repeated design, divinely fashioned by the same majestic Creator who made the Milky Way, Mount Everest, and the mighty proton.

My friend Laura marvels at the Lord's infinite mind, as I do. Over the last seventeen years, we've had many long talks about what it means to be God's women and Christ's followers. I'm going to miss her when she leaves the country next year to serve as a New Testament translator.

Last month Laura and her family relocated from Nebraska to Texas — the first of the final steps she will take before departing the States. She now lives in temporary housing with her husband, Matt, and their two teenage sons. They've applied for and received visas; their home has been leased to another family; most of their possessions have been sold, given away, placed in storage, or donated to Goodwill. Though all of these actions confirm my friend's faithful commitment to entering full-time Christian service abroad, it is the witness of her heart that most inspires me.

"Where we're going, there are no copies of the New Testament in a language that the people can understand," Laura told me. "The country has never been open to Christians, so it remains closed to traditional means of sharing the Gospel. But that doesn't mean the work can't be done. Based on what other Christian workers have told us about living in the area, we have a pretty clear understanding of what God wants us to do and how he wants us to do it."

After hearing Laura's words, it didn't take long for tears to fill my eyes as I tried to imagine what my own life would have been like over the last forty-six years without God's Word.

"Initially, we plan to go as tourists. Our visas will allow us to remain in the country for up to four years at a time. Matt's self-supporting profession should help us officially extend our stay. So as long as our health and finances allow, we'll continue with our translation work for as long as the Lord wants us to be there," Laura explained. "We'll get to know the people, the language and its idioms, the local customs."

When I asked Laura how long it usually takes to complete a translation of the New Testament under such conditions, she replied calmly, "About twenty years."

Twenty years! At first I thought I hadn't heard my friend's answer correctly. Finally it sunk in. She was telling me that she was willing to spend the best years of her adult life on a single project, thousands of miles away from family and friends, while surrounded by street stench and shamans.

"Twenty years?" I asked, more to hear the number again than to raise doubt about my friend's credibility.

"Yep."

I'll never forget Laura's face at that moment. I know my friend very well, and yet the ease of her reply surprised me. She appeared to be completely comfortable with the thought of living in a remote mountain region of southern Asia for as long as two decades even though she herself had grown up on a small family farm in Kansas.

As I stood in my kitchen with Laura, I had no doubts about her calling — or her spiritual fitness — regarding the challenging task ahead. I believe God has genuinely gifted my friend with a ministry of compassion, intercessory prayer, and spiritual discernment; I have seen the fruit of her service. That he is leading her to use these gifts on a mission field far from home is a beautiful testimony to the Lord's magnificent love for Laura.

"The resolute desire for women to know, be and develop themselves, and to use their gifts in the service of the world, is so obviously God's will for them, that to deny or frustrate it is an extremely serious oppression. It is a woman's basic right and responsibility to discover herself, her identity, and her vocation," explains evangelical theologian John Stott.[2]

"That women are called to ministry hardly needs any demonstration," he adds. "'Ministry' is 'service' (*diakonia*), and every Christian, male and female, young and old, is called to follow in the footsteps of him who said he had not come to be served, but to serve (Mark 10:45).... Our Christian doctrines of creation and redemption tell us that God wants his gifted people to be fulfilled, not frustrated, and his church to be enriched by their service."[3]

In these brief statements, John Stott reaffirms the traditional norms revealed both in Scripture and the lives of women in the early church. Laboring for the Lord — consecrating our lives to his service — is a privilege every woman may partake of in each day with gentle dignity. As we seek to serve our Savior and humbly live according to his unduplicatable design for our lives, we see that our self-worth is based on God's view of us, not on our own opinions or others' attitudes toward us. Our identity becomes securely centered in the reality of what Jesus has accomplished on our behalf, not on what we have accomplished for ourselves.

Peter wrote that as people of God we are "to proclaim the triumphs of him who has called you out of darkness into his marvelous light" (1 Peter 2:9 NEB). But proclaiming the Lord's love often requires a sacrifice of our personal ease. It takes courage and time and effort. And as the following verse from the old Celtic hymn "Be Thou My Vision" explains, it takes an ardent desire to view creation with the eyes of Christ:

Be Thou my vision, O Lord of my heart,
Naught be all else to me save that Thou art —
Thou my best thought, by day or by night,
Waking or sleeping, Thy presence my light.

— Old Celtic Hynm
Translated by Mary Byrne (1880–1931)
and Eleanor Hull (1860–1935)

Here I turn to two stories, the first of Deborah, a specially appointed judge of Israel, a prophetic visionary, who was able to keep her focus, obey God's commands, inspire ten thousand men to fight the Lord's war — and win. Then thousands of years later, in Britain, the second story provides glimpses into the life of Hannah More, an articulate Christian writer who found herself among the earliest of those who denounced slavery and sought to educate the poor.

Deborah's Story

After Joshua had brought the children of Israel into Canaan, Israel enjoyed peace and prosperity. But as the people's sense of security grew, they became less attentive to the Lord's laws — an often repeated pattern, as outlined in the Old Testament. And early victories in Canaan had resulted in a fatal error. Rather than zealously driving out the Canaanites and breaking down Canaan's altars as the Lord had directed, Israel's tribal leaders had struck political deals, forcing their people into slavery.

"I brought you up out of Egypt into this land that I swore to give to your ancestors, and I said I would never break my covenant with you," the angel of the Lord told them. "For your part, you were not to make any covenants with the people living in this land; instead, you were to destroy their altars. Why, then, have you disobeyed my command? Since you have done this, I will no longer drive out the people living in your land. They will be thorns in your sides, and their gods will be a constant temptation to you" (Judg. 2:1–2 NLB).

And they were. Cultural assimilation quickly followed the Israelites' disobedience to God's commands. In just one generation, forbidden intermarriages and pagan practices worked inside Israel's tribes like a terrible leaven. Their acceptance of Canaan's social customs came at a high price as the people of Israel lost their spiritual focus, forgot the

Lord, and practiced idolatry by serving Canaan's animistic gods, the Baals (Bulls) and the Asherahs (Cows).

The unholy cults were overseen by male and female priest-prostitutes with whom temple visitors regularly engaged in sexual relations as an act of religious worship. Because the Canaanites viewed the priests as the gods' and goddesses' select representatives, the people believed they could improve the fertility of crops, livestock, and women by having intercourse with the temple priests and priest-esses. This belief was utterly opposed by God's commandments and Jewish teaching — an abomination, according to Levitical law. Even so, the temple's temptations became a deadly snare for Hebrew men and women.

The Israelites' worship of false gods at open-air altars and behind the temples' closed doors provoked God to anger: "In his anger against Israel the Lord handed them over to raiders who plundered them. He sold them to their enemies all around, whom they were no longer able to resist. Whenever Israel went out to fight, the hand of the Lord was against them, to defeat them, just as he had sworn to them. They were in great distress" (Judg. 2:14–15).

In response to the people's cry for deliverance, "the Lord raised up judges to rescue the Israelites from their enemies" (Judg. 2:16 NLB), revealing the Lord's covenantal faithfulness to his flawed people. The judges, fourteen altogether, successively dealt with the national crises that followed each new cycle of disobedience and defilement. After Ehud's and Shamgar's period of rule, a woman named Deborah was called by God to serve Israel as one of these judges.

When Deborah came on the scene, the tribes of Israel were suffering greatly. Village life had ceased functioning. Women and children were not safe. Travel had become so dangerous that people had abandoned the main roads in favor of winding side paths. Business and trade had shut down. Jabin, a wealthy Canaanite king, had enslaved the Hebrew population for two decades; his cruel military commander, Sisera, continuously ravaged the countryside. Not a single shield or spear was to be seen among the forty thousand men of Israel's twelve tribes. Abraham's descendants were no longer the inspirers of envy or revenge — they were the demoralized, dispirited, and depressed objects of Canaan's scorn.

A Specially Selected Source of Help

> *You, O Lord, keep my lamp burning; my God turns my darkness into light.* Psalm 18:28

*I*srael's ongoing pattern of disobedience, alien oppression, cries for help, and God's sovereign deliverance had been repeated over and over again by the time we gain a glimpse of Deborah — wife, poet, prophetess, Israel's appointed leader, and its first and only female judge.

We first see her sitting under a palm tree, settling disputes. The tree, which came to be named for her — the Palm of Deborah — was located in the hill country of Ephraim, about eight miles north of what would one day be known as Jerusalem. She held court there, overlooking a rock-covered vista of shrubs and bluffs.

Gien Karssen notes: "Not all of the roads in the country were deserted. One was walked on quite frequently. . . . More and more people were going to a palm tree which stood plainly above the surrounding shrubbery."[4] For years, Deborah had decided countless cases, heard many anguished accounts. She'd held this position of respect for some time, long enough to be considered a leader of Israel (Judg. 4:4). Her experience had taught her discernment, patience, and compassion.

Hour after hour, sitting under the unrelenting sun and the small shelter of her towering palm tree, Deborah listened before she spoke. Presenting their cases before their judge, Israel's men and women were confident they would receive fair treatment. They accepted her lucid decisions with respect, if not always with gratitude. The Hebrews trusted Deborah's words because they believed she represented God's active interest in Israel. To them, Lappidoth's wife was the Lord's sole spokesperson.

Deborah was the only judge of Israel who would be called a *prophet* — a foreteller and forthteller, someone to whom God gave specific knowledge of future events and divinely inspired words of instruction and correction, who then made this information known publicly. She was also the only woman in Old Testament history who would rise to the pinnacle of political power by the people's common consent.

Though Deborah possessed no royal lineage, she led Israel, a nation with no precedent for a woman ruler, with the authentic confidence and grace of a great queen — and a true mother. "Deborah's highest title was a 'mother of Israel' (Judg. 5:7)," Edith Deen notes. "Her motherly function transcended the limits of her own home, so that in her love for her people, which was akin to her love for her children, she protected Israel and trained its people in the direction of greatness."[5]

Barak's Plea

> *With your help, I can advance against a troop; with my*
> *God I can scale a wall.* Psalm 18:29

Gifted. Called. Appointed. The prophetess sensed that it was time to move out and confront the Lord's enemies. One day she courageously summoned to her tree Barak, one of Israel's most adroit army leaders. (His name means "thunderous lightning.")

When he arrived from his home in the north, Deborah was ready to tell him her plan. "The Lord, the God of Israel, commands you: 'Go, take with you ten thousand men of Naphtali and Zebulun and lead the way to Mount Tabor. I will lure Sisera, the commander of Jabin's army, with his chariots and his troops to the Kishon River and give him into your hands'" (Judg. 4:6–7).

In Deborah's voice Barak heard an unwavering faith in God. In her eyes he saw a decisive godly wisdom, illuminated from within by the Spirit's holy fire.

Barak, a formidable, seasoned soldier, clearly heard the Lord's twofold promise — "I will lure Sisera ... and give him into your hands." Deborah had spoken it so persuasively, yes, prophetically. Her confidence, her lack of fear of the tyrannical Sisera and his nine hundred chariots of iron, prompted him to suddenly make one of the most unusual statements by any man in biblical history. "If you go with me, I will go," he said with transparent honesty, "but if you don't go with me, I won't go" (Judg. 4:8).

The irony didn't slip by her: thunderous Barak saying he'd go to war only if Deborah went with him. Deborah took his request in stride. She listened well and discerned no flattery in

Barak's statement, no pretense or coercion. Just the plain and simple truth.

"Very well, I will go with you," she replied. "But because of the way you are going about this, the honor will not be yours, for the Lord will hand Sisera over to a woman" (Judg. 4:9).

Barak flinched for a second, the words hitting his masculine pride. But he prized Israel's victory more than his ego and kept his request on the table. *If this is the Lord's condition for bringing down the Canaanite army, it means nothing compared to what it will mean to win our freedom from Jabin.* He wanted Deborah at his side, trusting her faith more than his own. Though he could not comprehend how the Lord would achieve victory through his army — with no horses or reliable weaponry — he gathered that army and acted on God's singular promise of Sisera's defeat.

March On, My Soul — Be Strong!

> *The Lord lives! Praise be to my Rock! Exalted by God my Savior! He is the God who avenges me, who subdues nations under me, who saves me from my enemies.* Psalm 18:46–48

Nothing dissuaded Deborah from her calling. She traveled north with Barak to Kedesh. She stood by as he summoned Israel's only willing warriors; she witnessed the assembly of a small army of ten thousand fighting men. Then she marched alongside Barak toward Mount Tabor, her presence emboldening Barak's soldiers, reminding them of God's covenant with Israel.

This battle would be no surprise to Sisera, who set up his artillery when forewarned by a nomad named Heber of Barak's maneuvers. Sisera's nine hundred iron chariots fitted with axle scythes were positioned and ready. The Canaanite military leader expected nothing less than the total annihilation of Israel's ill-equipped army.

But Sisera did not know about Deborah, whose dynamic service to her people and her ten thousand fighting men were fueled by God's supernatural strength — a force infinitely more powerful than any human effort or natural feat.

On the appointed day, Deborah heard an order from the Lord and passed it along to Barak: "Go! This is the day the Lord has given Sisera into your hands. Has not the Lord gone ahead of you?" (Judg. 4:14). Without hesitating, Barak led his ten thousand men to meet Sisera's army. None of Israel's warriors were well armed. None rode in chariots. Not one was trained for combat. Yet they marched on, gripping their crude implements of war, in the hope that God would grant them a miracle.

And he did. As Barak and his troops surged into battle, they were greeted by the terrifying spectacle of God's startling intervention. Storm clouds swirled violently. Torrential rain poured down, creating a vast sea of mud, trapping Sisera's chariots and horses. The flooded river Kishon blocked Sisera's only route of escape. If that weren't enough, sleet, hail, lightning, and a bone-chilling wind suddenly disoriented Sisera's doomed men, rendering them powerless to defend themselves against Barak's advancing militia. Later, Deborah described the horrific scene in a victory poem:

> *From the heavens the stars fought,*
> *from their courses they fought against Sisera.*
> *The river Kishon swept them away,*
> *the age-old river, the river Kishon.*
> *March on, my soul; be strong!*

—Judges 5:20–21

In Jael's Tent

> *I crushed them so that they could not rise;*
> *they fell beneath my feet.* Psalm 18:38

*N*one of the Canaanite men survived that heavenly and earthly battle except Sisera himself. Looking for a safe place to hide, he ran for his life.

His destination? The camp of Heber, the nomad who had tipped him off to Barak's mobilization. *I'll be safe there,* he told himself, *with Heber, a sympathizer.*

The first person he saw was Jael, Heber's wife, standing in the doorway of her tent. Ah, safety. She even was beckoning him to enter. Jael smiled. "Come, my lord, come right in. Don't be afraid" (Judg. 4:18). If he'd taken time to think, he would have realized this was an unusual request: Husband and father were the only men welcome in a woman's tent, and Sisera had a reputation for violating women. But Sisera didn't think twice. He was desperate: It was only a matter of time before Barak would come searching for him. What better hiding place could there possibly be than a woman's tent?

Sisera slid into the tent, caught his breath, and asked for a drink.

Jael opened a skin of milk, gave him a bowlful, and gently lay a cover over him to signify her hospitality. Just before he closed his eyes, sinking into a deep, dreamless sleep, Sisera noticed that Jael was still smiling.

As the wife of a desert nomad, it was Jael's responsibility to take down and put up the tents. This was one strong-armed woman, accustomed to driving the long stakes into the dry ground. Whether premeditated or spontaneous, we don't know, but once Sisera was fast asleep, Jael quietly crept over to pick up the familiar domestic implements. With one perfect stroke of her hammer, she drove a sharpened peg through Sisera's temple, crushing his skull and nailing him firmly to the ground.

When Barak arrived a short time later, Jael welcomed him also. "Come," she said, "and I will show you the man you're looking for" (Judg. 4:22).

Seeing Sisera's dead body, Barak knew the words of Deborah's prophecy had been fulfilled. He brought Deborah to his side and together they sang a song of victory and praise.

The Ode of Deborah

> *I pursued my enemies and overtook them; I did not turn back till they were destroyed.* Psalm 18:37

When the battle was over, Deborah wrote and sang one of the first known poems in Hebrew. It's a wonderful testament of God's power, of his hand in the victory. It starts and ends with praise to her Lord, and tells the story of the battle, naming the characters, praising the bravery of the soldiers and of Jael, naming herself but with some modesty as "a mother in Israel."

> *When the princes in Israel take the lead,*
> *when the people willingly offer themselves —*
> *praise the Lord!*
> *Hear this, you kings! Listen, you rulers!*
> *I will sing to the Lord, I will sing;*
> *I will make music to the Lord, the God of Israel.*

. . . .
In the days if Shamgar son of Anath,
  in the days of Jael, the roads were abandoned;
  travelers took to winding paths.
Village life in Israel ceased,
  ceased until I, Deborah, arose,
  arose a mother in Israel.
When they chose new gods,
  war came to the city gates,
and not a shield or spear was seen
  among forty thousand in Israel.
My heart is with Israel's princes,
  with the willing volunteers among the people.
  Praise the Lord!
. . . .
Then the people of the Lord
  went down to the city gates.
"Wake up, wake up, Deborah!
  Wake up, wake up, break out in song!
Arise, O Barak!
  Take captive your captives, O son of Abinoam."

Then the men who were left
  came down to the nobles;
the people of the Lord
  came to me with the mighty.
. . . .
Kings came, they fought;
  the kings of Canaan fought
at Tannach by the waters of Megiddo,
  but they carried off no silver, no plunder.
From the heavens the stars fought,
  from their courses they fought against Sisera.
The river Kishon swept them away,
  the age-old river, the river Kishon.
  March on, my soul; be strong!

. . . .
Most blessed of women be Jael,
  the wife of Heber the Kenite,
  most blessed of tent-dwelling women.
He asked for water, and she gave him milk;
  in a bowl fit for nobles she brought him curdled milk.
Her hand reached for the tent peg,
  her right hand for the workman's hammer.
She struck Sisera, she crushed his head,
  she shattered and pierced his temple.
At her feet he sank,
  he fell; there he lay.
At her feet he sank, he fell;
  where he sank, there he fell — dead.

Through the window peered Sisera's mother;
  behind the lattice she cried out,
"Why is his chariot so long in coming?
  Why is the clatter of his chariots delayed?"
The wisest of her ladies answer her;
  indeed, she keeps saying to herself,
"Are they not finding and dividing the spoils:
  a girl or two for each man,
  colorful garments as plunder for Sisera,
  colorful garments embroidered,
  highly embroidered garments for my neck —
all this as plunder?"

So may all your enemies perish, O Lord!
  But may they who love you be like the sun
  when it rises in strength.

—Judges 5:2–31

I love the ending of this song — Deborah's wonderful
image that those who love God are like the sun when it rises

in strength. Like the sun — so constant in its course, always moving ahead on a clear path, with a set vision, day upon day upon day.

Steve Mila

Hannah More's Story

Hannah More lived in England in the second half of the eighteenth century — a particularly troublesome but interesting time in history. She was fifteen when George III ascended the throne, thirty-one when the Declaration of Independence was signed, forty-four when French revolutionaries besieged the Bastille, seventy when Napoleon surrendered at Waterloo, and eighty-eight when Parliament first provided money toward public education in 1833.

Hannah was born in 1745 near Bristol, England, the fourth of five happy, resourceful daughters, the children of a schoolmaster and a farmer's daughter. She promptly learned to read by the age of three. Though her father permitted her to read Latin, he did not encourage any of his five daughters to study mathematics, believing the female brain physiologically incapable of retaining much academic learning — a widely held belief at that time. Not that that stopped adolescent Hannah, who enthusiastically maintained self-directed studies, helped along by her older sisters who ran a boarding school for young women. Though all five of the More daughters were widely regarded as "pious, intelligent, and highly competent," Hannah was precociously intelligent and came to be considered the brightest of them all.[6]

A childhood friend of Hannah, the writer Marianne Thornton, described Hannah's childhood home as a lovely place where "roses and haycocks and strawberries and syllabub and huge brown-baked loaves" greeted visitors. And she noted that the family's two beloved cats, Non-resistance and Passive Obedience, were pampered with delectable food treats. In the midst of this idyllic household sat Hannah, the storyteller; colorful versions of Old Testament stories were "told by Hannah with such eloquence and force that I fancied she must have lived amongst them herself."[7]

At age seventeen, Hannah published *A Search for Happiness*, followed by three acclaimed pastoral plays. Yet her writing and storytelling were often criticized — "This is not the sort of thing that proper young ladies do, Hannah" — and she was urged to improve herself by making puddings.

Hannah continued her writing efforts, later observing, "A Christian lives at the height of his being, not only at the top of his spiritual but of his intellectual life.... Let your soul act up to its high destination."[8]

Hannah's determination to fully employ her God-given gifts proved costly. An attractive and companionable woman, she was engaged to be married three times to the same man, a wealthy landowner named William Turner, twenty years her senior, with an estate near Bristol. Hannah had to repeatedly postpone the wedding to accommodate Mr. Turner's marital phobias. Her last betrothal, at the age of twenty-eight, ended in heartbreak: On the wedding day, Mr. Turner simply failed to show up, leaving a mortified Hannah waiting at the church. Though Hannah decided never to marry as a result of this painful experience, she was later respectfully referred to as *Mrs*. Hannah More.

Mr. Turner himself was embarrassed and, as recompense, he contacted Hannah's spiritual mentor and neighbor, the Rev. James Stonehouse. The two men made a confidential arrangement that provided Hannah a lifetime annuity of two hundred pounds a year. This generous settlement helped her to become, first, a prominent member of London's literary circle and, later, after her conversion, a Christian philanthropist, founder of public schools, and publisher of religious tracts against slavery.

Ministry in London

> *Love must be sincere. Hate what is evil; cling to what is good. Be devoted to one another in brotherly love. Honor one another above yourselves.* Romans 12:9–10

*W*hile Hannah's annuity certainly opened doors, her gift with words — as a playwright, author, and storyteller — secured her social connection with many of the premier literary and theatrical luminaries of her era.

Having moved to London shortly after the demise of her wedding plans when she was twenty-eight, Hannah was quickly accepted by many of the city's leading elite. Samuel Johnson, the wordsmith and eloquent leader of an eminent social circle, was so impressed with Hannah that he once called her "the most powerful versificatrix of the English language."[9] Others in the group included the painter Joshua Reynolds and his wife; Edmund Burke, the local parliamentarian; Eva and David Garrick, the foremost actor of his day; and physicist Isaac Newton.

Following one social visit in 1775, Hannah humorously observed in a letter to her sister:

> Our first visit was to Sir Joshua's, where we were received with all the friendship imaginable. I am going today, to a great dinner. Nothing can be conceived so absurd, extravagant, and fantastical, as the present mode of dressing the head. Simplicity and modesty are things so much exploded, that the very

192 ~ *Women of Courage*

names are no longer remembered. I have just escaped from one of the most fashionable disfigurers; and though I charged him to dress me with the greatest simplicity, and to have only a very distant eye upon fashion, just to avoid the pride of singularity, without running into ridiculous excess; yet in spite of all these sage didactics, I absolutely blush at myself, and turn to the glass with as much caution as a vain beauty, just risen from the smallpox; which cannot be a more disfiguring disease than the present mode of dressing.[10]

As impressive as Hannah's dazzling verbal skills and writing were, it wasn't her formidable talent that won her friends' true devotion — it was her heart. After David Garrick died, Hannah spent long days consoling his widow. At the end of his life, Samuel Johnson had Hannah accompany him on his final trip to church for Communion. When Oxford professor Benjamin Kennicott, who had spent thirty years assembling the Old Testament, lay dying, Mrs. Kennicott called upon Hannah for steady spiritual support.

By age thirty-five, Hannah had grown restless. Something was missing. Writing plays, poetry, and stories no longer brought personal satisfaction. Sensing the need for a true revival, she felt increasingly uncomfortable with the superficiality of "respectable" religion in London. A spiritual restlessness — sensing that her hunger for fame, recognition, and success was inconsistent with her faith commitment — led Hannah to seek pastoral help. John Newton, the one-time slave trader who memorialized his conversion by writing "Amazing Grace," was now pastor of a vibrant London church. After reading a book of his, Hannah sought him out and asked him to serve as her pastoral adviser.

The Small Group at Clapham

Share with God's people who are in need.
Practice hospitality. Romans 12:13

Through John Newton, Hannah made the acquaintance of an entirely different, but equally influential, set of friends, centrally William Wilberforce. Wilberforce was a very young parliamentarian who seemed destined to become prime minister. But after committing himself to Christ at age twenty-five, he felt called to stay in Parliament and work toward two goals: "God Almighty has put before me two great objects — the abolition of the slave trade and the reformation of the manners of England."[11]

In the *Memoir of Wilberforce,* published only three years after Wilberforce's death, his biographer wrote, "One who knew him well tells us that few members attended with more assiduity in their places in parliament. Though his frame was always weak, and his health indifferent, he rarely absented himself from public duty: he had, indeed, a higher motive to its discharge than most men. Though singularly destitute of self-importance, he was sensible that he had gradually risen to a peculiar responsibility, which there were few, if any, to share with him."[12]

Herself newly recommitted to Christ, Hannah received the additional privilege of lasting friendship with this remarkable man. She soon caught Wilberforce's vision, and for the rest of her life devoted the bulk of her resources — spiritual, physical, intellectual, emotional, and financial — to fighting slavery, poverty, and illiteracy. Along with Wilberforce, Hannah became an instrumental member of a small group of Bible-believing Christians living near Clapham, an affluent suburb of London. The group, which included John Newton and two bishops, earnestly applied itself to prayer, Bible study, and good works throughout Great Britain.

"In Parliament, during their lifetimes, they were lampooned as 'The Saints,' and in history they have been remembered as 'The Clapham Sect,'" Ernest Marshall Howse explains in *Saints in Politics*. "By the liberality of their minds no less than their purses, by their chosen causes, their concerted labors, their systematic research, their original methods of organizing public opinion, their persistent and triumphant campaigns, they made a permanent difference to not only the history of England but of the modern world."[13]

The Clapham Sect formally began in 1765 and gradually developed a true Christian kinship, "knit together in an astonishing intimacy and solidarity."[14] Many of its members owned magnificent houses located in close proximity, friends as well as neighbors; marriage among the families associated with the group grew increasingly commonplace. Hannah, welcomed into the group nearly twenty years after its inception, became part of "the second generation of Claphamites." Four were knighted. In time, Hannah became the appointed agent of Wilberforce and others in their philanthropic activities, causing one historian to observe, "Equally with Wilberforce and [Charles] Simeon, she was one of the 'great men' of the party."[15]

With her increasing involvement in the Clapham Sect and relocation to a new home, Hannah's writing grew more inspired. She gave up her London home and frequently found spiritual refreshment in the wooded hills of Sussex at a rural cottage called Cowslip Green. "To maintain a devotional spirit, two things are especially necessary: to cultivate the disposition and to avoid whatever is unfavorable to it," Hannah observed. "Frequent retirement and recollection are indispensable, together with such a general course of reading as will help maintain it."[16] She valued the quiet, but she still welcomed the outside world, frequently entertaining "nobility, bishops, poets and a host of others."[17]

Her well-reasoned writings exposing the horrors of the slave trade were widely distributed and critically influential. One poem about the abolition of slavery in Ceylon was set to music by Charles Wesley. Her series of *Sacred Dramas* addressed additional moral controversies. With the Clapham Sect underwriting all publication expenses, Hannah wrote Christian tracts, many in a series created in response to the French Revolution, and many given away free.

Hannah and Her Sisters

> *Live in harmony with one another. Do not be proud, but be willing to associate with people of low position. Do not be conceited.* Romans 12:16

Hannah's expansive vision for ministry was continually unfolding. "Where there is no vision, the people perish: but he that keepeth the law, happy is he," King Solomon wisely observed (Prov. 29:18 KJV). As Hannah continued to commit herself to the Lord's work, she saw new opportunities to serve Christ among the poor, the homeless, the illiterate — and the aristocracy.

One day in 1789, Hannah accompanied William Wilberforce on a tour of a mining district in Cheddar, near Bristol, where homeless people eeked out an existence living in caves and cliffs. Appalled by the suffering, Wilberforce turned to his friend and said quietly and firmly: "Miss Hannah, something must be done for Cheddar."

Equally horrified by the poverty, Hannah opened her heart and set out on a courageous mission; together this brother and sister in Christ launched an extensive educational crusade for children and adults. Hannah's sisters also joined the team, with Wilberforce providing funds to start Sunday schools in poor mining villages to give children a spiritual and secular education — a truly visionary concept at that time.

Hannah's classes — some meeting in barns — met with resistance from the local farmers and some clergy, who voiced their concerns about losing control over the poor. What's more, the poor were being led by *women*.

But, like "mother Deborah" before her, Hannah and her sisters would not be dissuaded. Hannah personally oversaw the distribution of clothing, Testaments, tracts, and prayer books. She founded a home economics school for girls, started mothers' clubs to aid women in caring for their children during sickness and distress, and spent much of her time training new teachers. Neglected elderly people from almshouses stopped by, also receiving encouragement and support.

In 1793, when Hannah held an Annual School Feast in the city of Bath, the local newspaper reported that nearly a thousand children from nine Sunday schools picnicked on "beef, bread pudding, and cyder."[18] For Hannah, faith and works went hand in hand:

> *If faith produce no works, I see*
> *That faith is not a living tree.*
> *Thus faith and works together grow;*
> *No separate life they e'er can know:*
> *They're soul and body, hand and heart:*
> *What God hath joined, let no man part.*[19]

Hannah's Final Years

Bless those who persecute you; bless and do not curse.
Rejoice with those who rejoice; mourn with those who
mourn. Romans 12:14–15

Hannah was notably ahead of her time in a number of important areas. As a single woman serving the Lord in full-time ministry, she graciously paved a path for other Christian women to follow, not in a convent, but in her community and church. Among the members of her small group, which was a precursor to our modern-day small-group church movement, she was regarded as a contributing peer and an anointed leader.

"By her own pen she ... [produced] moral tracts that sold in [the] millions in Britain, America and other parts of the English-speaking world," explain Jeremy and Margaret Collingwood in a recent biography. "Through her pioneer work in the schools ... she set in motion a whole new programme of popular education, and gave literacy and dignity to thousands of poor children.... It made no difference to her whether her pupils were the scruffiest and poorest children of Mendip miners or the leaders of society. To each she gave herself without reserve. Hannah became one of the major driving forces in teaching the nation to read."[20]

Hannah's gifts as a writer, remarkable as they were, were especially noteworthy because she did not often disguise her identity by signing her works with a masculine pseudonym or "Anonymous," as did her contemporaries George Eliot (Mary Ann Evans) and Jane Austen. Her willingness to publish most of her plays, poems, and novels under her own name — a woman's name — gives us insight into her personal integrity.

Hannah was a trailblazer in another important way: by continuing to write, publish, and practice Christian philanthropy during her later years, she showed that advancing age does not necessarily diminish a woman's God-given capacity to pray, think, teach, counsel, create, nourish, and influence others.

Although Hannah suffered from chronic asthma, allergies, bronchitis, and other ailments that forced her to leave her home each winter, she survived her sisters by more than ten years. In her final years she spent many days in bed. Yet she kept writing, counseling, and ministering to the poor until the end. Her last books — *An Essay on the Character of Saint Paul, An Estimate of the Religion of the Fashionable World*, and, finally, *The Spirit of Prayer*, a contemplative anthology selected from her previous work — ranked among her best. Two centuries later, her words remain fresh, passionate, and real, somewhat reminiscent of another famous British Anglican, C. S. Lewis.

Here I give you a sampling — some of my favorites, which again draw my attention to her clear focus and vision:

> If God be the centre to which our hearts are tending, every line in our lives must meet in Him. With this point in view there will be a harmony between our prayers and our practice, a consistency between devotion and conduct, which will make every part turn to this one end, bear upon this one point. For the beauty of the Christian [life] consists not in parts (however good in themselves) which tend to separate views and lead to different ends; but it arises from its being one intact, uniform, connected plan.... The design of prayer, therefore, as we have observed, is not merely to make us devout while we are engaged

in it, but that its [fragrance] may be diffused through all the intermediate spaces of the day, enter into all its occupations, duties and tempers.[21]

The great, the only effectual antidote to self-love is to get the love of God and of our neighbor firmly rooted in the heart. Yet let us ever bear in mind that dependence on our fellow-creatures is as carefully to be avoided as love of them is to be cultivated. There is none but God on whom the principles of love and dependence form but one duty. . . .

Christianity . . . is not a religion of forms, modes, and decencies. It is being transformed into the image of God. It is being like-minded with Christ. It is considering Him our sanctification as well as our redemption. It is endeavoring to live with Him here, that we may live with Him hereafter. It is desiring earnestly to surrender our will to His, our heart to the conduct of His Spirit, our life to the guidance of His Word.[22]

The prophets and apostles were not deterred from pouring out the overflowings of their fervent spirits, they were not restrained from celebrating the perfections of their Creator, through the cold-hearted fear of being reckoned enthusiasts. The saints of old were not prevented from breathing out their rapturous hosannahs to the King of Saints, through the cowardly dread of being branded as fanatical. The conceptions of their minds [expanded] with the view of the glorious constellation of the Divine attributes; and the affections of their hearts warming with the thought, that those attributes were all concentrated in mercy.[23]

The passage of time has not diminished the witness of Hannah's eloquent words. Her writing and her story stand before us, unshaken by cultural upheaval and history's travails, as a lasting legacy — a shining testament concerning her most profound convictions about loving God.

When we look back upon the lives of Hannah More and William Wilberforce, it is not surprising to discover that they shared a common end: After forty-five years of actively praying and fighting to win the emancipation of all slaves, their final victory was achieved in 1833 when Parliament passed a bill abolishing slavery throughout the British Empire. Seven hundred thousand slaves were given their freedom. In the same year, God called both Hannah and William home to be with their Lord.

When Hannah died, some two hundred schoolchildren accompanied her casket down the city streets; crowds gathered to pay respect to Bristol's beloved Christian hero. She bequeathed all the money she had made through writing — said to be thirty thousand pounds, a considerable fortune in those days — to seventy charities and church societies, as well as to her local church. Hannah was buried alongside the remains of her sisters in a small family plot.

"No woman in England or the United States ever occupied such an exalted position or exercised such a broad or deep influence on the public mind in the combined character of woman of society, author and philanthropist," noted historian John Lord.[24] Her reputation is remembered, and for good reason: Hannah More had a matchless dynamic vision for what it means to be Christ's devoted, courageous disciple in a hurting world — for what she sagaciously called "the religion of the heart."

Who is on the Lord's side?
Who will serve the King?
Who will be His helpers,
Other lives to bring?
Who will leave the world's side?
Who will face the foe?
Who is on the Lord's side?
Who for Him will go?
By Thy call of mercy,
By Thy grace divine,
We are on the Lord's side,
Savior, we are Thine.

Not for weight of glory,
Not for crown and palm,
Enter we the army,
Raise the warrior psalm;
But for love that claimeth
Lives for whom He died;
He whom Jesus nameth
Must be on His side.
By Thy love constraining,
By Thy grace divine,
We are on the Lord's side,
Savior, we are Thine.

Fierce may be the conflict,
Strong may be the foe,
But the King's own army
None can overthrow.
Round His standard ranging;
Vict'ry is secure;
For His truth unchanging
Makes the triumph sure.
Joyfully enlisting
By Thy grace divine,
We are on the Lord's side,
Savior, we are Thine.

— Frances Ridley Havergal (1836–1879)

Conclusion

❧

*V*ision. A certain way of seeing. The ability to unflinchingly look at the big picture without becoming distracted by myriad minute details. Deborah had this God-given capacity; so did Hannah More. Each had a singleness of eye, a faithful clarity of focus that firmly fixed their mental, emotional, and spiritual concentration upon one supreme life purpose in spite of heavy opposition from their enemies. And their critics.

Dietrich Bonhoeffer, a German theologian and twentieth-century Christian martyr, said, "The life of discipleship can only be maintained as long as nothing is allowed to come between Christ and ourselves — neither the law, nor personal piety, nor even the world. The disciple always looks only to his master, never to Christ and the law, Christ and religion, Christ and the world. He avoids all such notions like the plague. Only by following Christ alone can he preserve a single eye. His eye rests wholly on the light that comes from Christ, and has no darkness or ambiguity in it."[25]

It's a fact: God has planted eternity in every human heart (Eccl. 3:11). A sideways glance can easily pull our attention away from the most important — and valuable — things in Christ's kingdom.

Bonhoeffer continues: "As the eye must be single, clear and pure in order to keep light in the body, as hand and foot can receive light from no other source save the eye, as the foot stumbles and the hand misses its mark when the eye is dim, as the whole body is in darkness when the eye is blind; so the follower of Christ is in the light only so long as he looks simply to Christ and at nothing else in the world."[26]

A momentary distraction, once it dominates our vision, can turn into a full-blown fixation. Roadside distractions can lead to destructive detours on dangerous paths.

But — alleluia! — our journey doesn't end if we misstep. Our tenderhearted Shepherd excels in divinely ministering to our wounded hearts and broken spirits when we get side-tracked. When pride sometimes causes us to lose our way. When temptation occasionally causes us to turn our eyes away from the Lord's loving gaze. When we momentarily lose our vision of the King's grand plan for our lives.

Like Deborah and Hannah, we need not get distracted in the face of our enemies or our opposition. Like them, we aren't infallible. We can't see God's plan with 100 percent accuracy. But these two women demonstrated with their lives the truth of Solomon's wise proverb: "Where there is no vision, the people perish: but he who keepeth the law, happy is he" (Prov. 29:18 KJV). Deborah's vision helped save her nation, while Hannah's helped solve the social and spiritual problems of her time.

No, we are not saved by our works, but as Hannah noted, we are called to courageously serve with clear vision, as my friend Laura and countless other Christian women are doing today. Perhaps the Lord is telling you to quit a job you love and stay home and raise children — or go on the mission field; perhaps he is asking you to work in a crisis pregnancy center or a shelter for abused and battered women; perhaps he is calling you to develop a deeper prayer life or spend more time alone with him; or perhaps he is calling you to minister to the elderly in a local nursing home or in your neighborhood. Sharing his love often requires a sacrifice of our personal ease. Though it takes courage and time and effort to "see" all of life from the perspective of eternity, it's worth it.

"You are the world's light.... Don't hide your light! Let it shine for all; let your good deeds glow for all to see, so that they may praise your heavenly Father" (Matt. 5:14–16 LB). Jesus proclaimed these words from a hilltop, not a sanctuary, dressed in simple garments, not priestly robes. Fixing our eyes on him, we cannot help but see the needs around us with new eyes.

We live in a hurting world filled with lonely and wounded and afflicted people. As a woman of God, are you willing to "set your mind on things above" and embrace God's kingly vision for your life? Are you willing to be like a city on a hill, glowing in the night with his light, for all to see?

Points for Reflection

1. The greatest distractions to seeing and hearing the Lord with my spiritual eyes and ears are . . .

2. Looking to Christ — setting my heart on the Lord alone — requires . . .

3. Deborah's vision of God and his will for her life demanded . . .

4. To limit the distractions that diminish, alter, or otherwise obscure my spiritual vision, I need . . .

5. Hannah More's involvement in the troubles of her nation reminds me of Deborah's story because . . .

6. When my vision of the Lord's design for my life is clearest, I see . . .

Prayer: Lord, from the heights of heaven You descended into human flesh to bring the light of Your life to me. You opened my eyes to realms of glory through a Cross, announcing pardon and hope, freedom and forgiveness, to all who believe. Jesus, I thank You! Shine through me, Lord, as I proclaim Your victory and bear witness to Your love. I rejoice in Your gift to me! Jesus, I place my life in Your hands. Amen.

Great things thou hast done,
    O Lord my God;
thy wonderful purposes are all for our good;
    none can compare with thee;
I would proclaim them and speak of them,
    but they are more than I can tell.

If thou hadst desired sacrifice and offering
    thou wouldst have given me ears to hear.
If thou hadst asked for whole-offering and sin-offering
    I would have said, "Here I am."
My desire is to do thy will, O God,
    and thy law is in my heart.

In the great assembly I have proclaimed what is right,
    I do not hold back my words,
    as thou knowest, O Lord.
I have not kept thy goodness hidden in my heart;
    I have proclaimed thy faithfulness and saving power,
and not concealed thy unfailing love and truth
    from the great assembly.

Thou, O Lord, dost not withhold
    thy tender care from me;
    thy unfailing love and truth for ever guard me.

— Psalm 40:5–11 NEB

Do not look at someone else and say — Well, if he can have those views and prosper, why cannot I? You have to walk in the light of the vision that has been given to you and not compare yourself with others or judge them, that is between them and God.[27]

— Oswald Chambers (1874–1917)

Come, thou bright and morning star,
Light of light without beginning,
Shine upon us from afar,
Like the morn when mists are thinning;
Drive away by thy clear light
Our dark night.

Let thy grace, like morning dew
Falling on the barren places,
Comfort, quicken, and renew
All dry souls and drying graces;
Bless thy rock from thy rich store
Evermore.

May thy fervent love destroy
All cold works in us awaking
Ardent courage, zeal, and joy,
At the purple morn's first breaking;
Let us rise, ere yet
Life has set.

Light us to the heavenly spheres,
Sun of grace, in glory shrouded;
Lead us through this vale of tears,
To the land where days unclouded,
Purest joy and perfect peace,
Never cease.

— C. Knorr, Baron von Rosenroth (1636–1689)
Translated by R. Massie (1857)

Closing Thoughts

Courage is what it takes to stand up and speak; courage is also what it takes to sit down and listen.

— Anonymous

The heart is deceitful above all things. . . . Who can understand it? I the Lord search the heart and examine the mind," God tells us through Jeremiah, the prophet (Jer. 17:9–10). On the surface, it's easy to be fooled into thinking our needs can be met in worldly pursuits or in people. But careers invariably come to an end. People consistently fail to meet our expectations. Dreams regularly fade away in the daylight.

If we try to find our identity in, or fix our vision on, these things rather than on Christ, our hearts remain restless, our arms vacant, our thoughts unfocused.

It can be remarkably humbling when we realize (for what may seem like the zillionth time) that only the Lord can satisfy our innermost desires. Nevertheless, we can courageously choose — over and over again: We can open our hearts to the Word of God. We can stretch out our empty arms to embrace our loving Redeemer. We can sit down and surrender our distracting thoughts to receive the quiet stillness of the Holy Spirit's presence — and, when the time is right, stand up and be prepared for action.

For the hungry, the empty, and the distracted, the message of Christ is the same. Jesus speaks of pardon and forgiveness, of joy and peace, given freely to all who look to him alone to satisfy their needs. "I am the light of the world" is the heart cry of our Savior. "Whoever follows me will never walk in darkness, but will have the light of life" (John 8:12). Are you trusting him today? Can you believe that he is bringing you ever closer to being fully conformed to the image of his Son? We can live in hopeful expectation of that day knowing that he will complete the work he has begun:

> Praise be to the God and Father of our Lord Jesus Christ, who in his great mercy gave us new birth into a living hope by the resurrection of Jesus Christ from the dead! The inheritance into which we are born is one that nothing can destroy or spoil or wither. It is kept for you in heaven, and you, because you put your faith in God, are under the protection of his power until salvation comes — the salvation which is even now in readiness and will be revealed at the end of time.... Fix your hopes on the gift of grace which is to be yours when Jesus Christ is revealed. (1 Peter 1:3–5, 13 NEB)

Living in the reality of this great truth with courage and grace is possible for all of us. As Christian women today we aren't called to face an executioner's sword, but we can draw strength from the story of a real woman who had the courage and the grace to face such a test.

For all of us, there are seasons of life. But for women the seasons tend to be more clearly marked. I've selected a variety of characters to show that no matter where we happen to be right now, there's no need to give up. If these women coped with the great obstacles in their lives and societies, so can we. Living out the Christian faith is possible for all of us. Everyone has a role and a gift to offer.

Through the ages, there have been many women with stories we can look back upon and remember, reflect on and be inspired by. In *Women of Courage*, you have read portrayals of twelve courageous women overcoming challenges from biblical times to the twentieth century. The six themes discussed in this book — faith, love, patience, humility, vocation, and vision — are ones we don't often see openly reflected in contemporary "accomplished" role models on television or in the media.

One of my goals in writing about these heroines of our faith was to bridge the distance between the people in the Bible and the people of today, to inspire readers with the stories of ordinary women who courageously confronted extraordinary challenges and hardships. To provide additional heroes in an era that commonly equates a woman's success with the amount of money she earns, the way she looks, the house she lives in, the car she drives.

The "average" woman today is called upon to balance career, church, and community involvement with the changing needs of her family and friends. Though we talk about the vanishing myth of the superwoman, her specter can still suddenly appear when we lose focus of our central calling by taking on too much — or, to be more specific, too many of the wrong things — too fast. Thankfully, on any given day, God promises to meet us where we are and never give us more than we can handle. Life is a separate walk for each of us. And, while we suffer when we try to compare ourselves with others, we can learn from observing.

It was my intent to bring these brave women of the past vividly back to life and share their success stories, to show how the Lord cared for them, guided their steps, revived their hearts, and brought them courage just when they needed it. Learning more about these twelve women has made their witness part of my life: I often find pieces of their stories popping up in my mind at unexpected moments, reminders not only of what God has done in the past, but what he is doing in my life today. It's my prayer that reading this book will do the same for you.

As women who have been transformed by the light of Christ, may we place our heart's focus on the same Lord who appeared before Anna in the temple and sat alongside the Samaritan woman at the well, who kept Mary of Egypt safe in the desert and filled the life of Catherine of Genoa with the satisfying sustenance of his supreme love.

As believers who have found our character and identity in the image of our Creator, as Priscilla and Hilda did, may we courageously trust in the one true God who directs our paths and is intimately acquainted with all our ways — the One who has declared himself "the same yesterday and today and forever" (Heb. 13:8) — the God of Abraham who powerfully led Deborah to miraculous victory and crowned Esther with lasting honor.

Like Hagar and Crispina, may we gain enlightening encouragement from knowing our heavenly Father is the God who sees, no matter how dark our surroundings may appear. Like Rosa and Hannah, may we feel Christ's concern and compassion for the oppressed as we follow his leading, one step at a time.

Let us join our voices with the everlasting chorus of the saints who have lived and died since Jesus' time, expectantly looking forward to the day when we will see our Savior face to face at last. "And so we will be with the Lord forever. Therefore encourage one another with these words" (1 Thess. 4:17–18).

Lord, hear our prayer!

How firm a foundation, ye saints of the Lord,
Is laid for our faith in his excellent word!
What more can he say than to you he hath said,
To you that for refuge to Jesus have fled?

Fear not, I am with thee; O be not dismayed!
For I am thy God, and will still give thee aid;
I'll strengthen thee, help thee, and cause thee to stand,
Upheld by my righteous, omnipotent hand.

When through the deep waters I call thee to go,
The rivers of woe shall not thee overflow;
For I will be with thee, thy troubles to bless,
And sanctify to thee thy deepest distress.

When through fiery trials thy pathway shall lie,
My grace, all-sufficient, shall be thy supply;
The flame shall not hurt thee; I only design
Thy dross to consume, and thy gold to refine.

The soul that to Jesus hath fled for repose,
I will not, I will not, desert to his foes;
That soul, though all hell shall endeavor to shake,
I'll never, no, never, no, never forsake.

— John Rippon (1751–1836)

Introduction

1. Amy Carmichael, *Whispers of His Power* (Old Tappan, N.J.: Fleming H. Revell, 1982), 106.
2. John White, *The Fight* (Downers Grove, Ill.: InterVarsity Press, 1976), 110.
3. Eugene Peterson, *A Long Obedience in the Same Direction* (Downers Grove, Ill.: InterVarsity Press, 1980), 150.

Chapter One: By Faith

1. Theodore L. Cuyler, quoted in *The Christian's Treasury*, Lissa Roche, ed. (Wheaton, Ill.: Crossway, 1995), 71.
2. Sheila Walsh, *Bring Back the Joy* (Grand Rapids: Zondervan, 1998), 108.
3. Philip Neri, quoted in *The Wisdom of the Saints*, Jill Haak Adels, ed. (New York: Oxford University Press, 1987), 58.
4. John Henry Newman, quoted in *The Doubleday Christian Quotation Collection*, Hannah Ward and Jennifer Wild, compilers (New York: Doubleday, 1997), 185.
5. Robert Southwell, quoted in Adels, *Wisdom of the Saints*, 79.
6. Herbert Mursurillo, *The Acts of the Christian Martyrs* (Oxford: Clarendon, 1972).
7. Sources for Crispina's story: Bruno Chenu et al., *The Book of Christian Martyrs* (New York: Crossroad, 1990); "The Martyrdom of Crispina," *In Her Own Words*, Amy Oden, ed. (Nashville: Abingdon, 1994), 44–46; Jill Evans, *Beloved and Chosen* (Norwich: Canterbury, 1993), 30–31; Donald Attwater, *The Avenel Dictionary of Saints* (New York: Avenel, 1965), 94–95; David Hugh Farmer, *The Oxford Dictionary of Saints*, 3rd. ed. (Oxford: Oxford University Press, 1992), 114–15.
8. Duane W. H. Arnold, trans., *Prayers of the Martyrs* (Grand Rapids: Zondervan, 1991), 24.
9. Charles Haddon Spurgeon, quoted in *Companions for the Soul*, Robert R. Hudson and Shelley Townsend-Hudson, eds. (Grand Rapids: Zondervan, 1995), September 8 selection.
10. Margaret Clarkson, *Grace Grows Best in Winter* (Grand Rapids: Eerdmans, 1984), 40–41.
11. Catherine Marshall, quoted in Ward and Wild, *Doubleday Christian Quotation Collection*, 20.

12. Christina Rossetti, *Goblin Market and Other Poems* (London: Macmillan, 1862), 128–29.

Chapter Two: For Love

1. Blaise Pascal, quoted in *12,000 Religious Quotations*, Frank S. Mead, ed. (Grand Rapids: Baker, 1989), 283.
2. Bernard of Clairvaux, quoted in *Devotional Classics*, Richard J. Foster and Bryan James Smith, eds. (San Francisco: Harper, 1990), 40.
3. Frederich von Hügel, *The Mystical Element of Religion As Studied in Saint Catherine of Genoa and Her Friends*, vol. 1 (London: J. M. Dent, 1908), 105.
4. *The Life and Sayings of St. Catherine of Genoa*, Paul Garvin, trans. and ed. (Staten Island, N.Y.: Alba, 1964), 25.
5. Catherine of Genoa, *The Spiritual Dialogue*, Serge Hughes, trans. (Mahwah, N.J.: Paulist Press, 1979), 132.
6. Hügel, *Mystical Element of Religion*, 159.
7. Garvin, *Life and Sayings of St. Catherine of Genoa*, 58.
8. Robert Ellsberg, *All Saints* (New York: Crossroad, 1997), 401.
9. Oswald Chambers, *My Utmost for His Highest* (New York: Dodd, Mead, 1935), 67.
10. *The Life and Doctrine of Saint Catherine of Genoa* (New York: Catholic Publication Society, 1874), 278.
11. C. S. Lewis, *George MacDonald: An Anthology* (London: Fount, 1983), 60.

Chapter Three: In Patience

1. *The Life and Doctrine of Saint Catherine of Genoa* (New York: Catholic Publication Society, 1874), 244.
2. Andrew Murray, *Abide in Christ* (Old Tappan, N.J.: Spire/Fleming H. Revell; n.d.), 23.
3. Ibid., 104-5.
4. Eugenia Price, *The Unique World of Women*, as quoted in Gien Karssen, *Her Name Is Woman*, bk. 1 (Colorado Springs: NavPress, 1975), 149.
5. Jean-Pierre de Caussade, *Self-Abandonment to Divine Providence* (Springfield, Ill.: Templegate, 1959), 5.
6. Augustine of Hippo, quoted in *The Joy of the Saints*, Robert Llewelyn, ed. (Springfield, Ill.: Templegate, 1988), 148.
7. Richard Hendrix, quoted in Ben Patterson, *Waiting: Finding Hope When God Seems Silent* (Downers Grove, Ill.: InterVarsity Press, 1989), 7.
8. Phyllis McGinley, *Saint Watching* (New York: Crossroad, 1989), 6.
9. Cyprian, quoted in *The Wisdom of the Saints*, Jill Haak Adels, ed. (New York: Oxford University Press, 1987), 43.
10. Mary of Egypt, quoted in *The Lives of the Saints*, Omer Engelbert, ed. (New York: Barnes & Noble, 1994), 129.
11. Mary of Egypt, quoted in *The Doubleday Christian Quotation Collection*, Hannah Ward and Jennifer Wild, compilers (New York: Doubleday, 1997), 35.
12. Kathleen Norris, *Cloister Walk* (New York: Riverhead, 1996), 165.

13. Mary of Egypt, quoted in Jill Evans, *Beloved and Chosen* (Norwich, Norfolk, Great Britain: Canterbury Press, 1993), 39.

14. *Daily Readings with the Desert Fathers*, Benedicta Ward, ed. (Springfield, Ill.: Templegate, 1990), 12.

15. Ibid., 13.

16. Guerric of Igny, quoted in ibid., 162.

17. Michael Downey, *Trappist: Living in the Land of Desire* (New York: Paulist Press, 1997), 163.

18. Elizabeth of the Trinity, quoted in *Doubleday Christian Quotation Collection*, Ward and Wild, 172.

19. Oswald Chambers, *My Utmost for His Highest* (New York: Dodd, Mead, 1935), 129.

Chapter Four: With Humble Confidence

1. Francis de Sales, quoted in *The Joy of the Saints*, Robert Llewelyn, ed. (Springfield, Ill.: Templegate, 1988), 24.

2. Frederick Buechner, *Wishful Thinking* (New York: Harper & Row, 1973), 40.

3. Dag Hammarskjöld, *Markings* (New York: Alfred A. Knopf, 1970), 174.

4. William Temple, *Christ in His Church* (London: Macmillan, 1925), 145.

5. Dietrich Bonhoeffer, quoted in Eugene H. Peterson, *A Long Obedience in the Same Direction* (Downers Grove, Ill.: InterVarsity Press, 1980), 32.

6. Carl Henry, quoted in Charles Colson, *Loving God* (Grand Rapids: Zondervan, 1983), 167.

7. Rosa Parks, *Quiet Strength* (Grand Rapids: Zondervan, 1994), 23.

8. Ibid., 22.

9. Ibid., 17–18.

10. Ibid., 23.

11. Ibid., 17.

12. Ibid., 23–24.

13. Ibid., 24.

14. Ibid., 42.

15. Ibid., 43.

16. Isaac of Syria, quoted in *Joy of the Saints*, Llewelyn, 31.

17. Ibid.

18. Florence Nightingale, quoted in *The Christian's Treasury*, Lissa Roche, ed. (Wheaton, Ill.: Crossway, 1995), 38.

19. George MacDonald, "The Disciple, XXVIII," *A Hidden Life and Other Poems* (New York: Scribner, Armstrong, 1872), 127–28.

Chapter Five: Through Vocation

1. Elisabeth Elliot, *These Strange Ashes* (New York: Harper & Row, 1975), 132.

2. Tryon Edwards, quoted in *On Being Christian*, Armand Eisen, ed. (Kansas City: Ariel/Andrews and McMeel, 1995), 31.

3. Elton Trueblood, *The Company of the Committed* (New York: Harper & Row, 1961), 32.

4. Gien Karssen, *Her Name Is Woman*, bk. 1 (Colorado Springs: NavPress, 1975), 195.

5. Jo Berry, *The Priscilla Principle* (Grand Rapids: Zondervan, 1984), 56.

6. Virginia Stem Owens, *Daughters of Eve* (Colorado Springs: NavPress, 1995), 217.

7. Bede, *A History of the English Church and Its People* (London: Penguin Classics, 1955), 115.

8. Jonathan Edwards, quoted in *Devotional Classics*, Richard J. Foster and Bryan James Smith, eds. (San Francisco: Harper, 1990), 20.

9. Ruth Tucker and Walter L. Liefeld, *Daughters of the Church* (Grand Rapids: Zondervan, 1987), 135.

10. Bede, *History of the English Church*, 247.

11. Edith Deen, *Great Women of the Christian Faith* (Urichsville, Ohio: Barbour, reprinted by arrangement with Harper & Row, 1959), 248.

12. David Hugh Farmer, *The Oxford Dictionary of Saints*, 3rd ed. (Oxford: Oxford University Press, 1992), 154.

13. Phillips Brooks, quoted in John Bartlett, *Familiar Quotations*, 15th ed. (Boston: Little, Brown, 1980), 619.

14. Quoted in Elisabeth Elliot, *Gateway to Joy* (Ann Arbor, Mich.: Servant, 1998), 113.

15. Corrie ten Boom, quoted in *The Doubleday Collection of Christian Quotations*, Hannah Ward and Jennifer Wild, compilers (New York: Doubleday, 1997), 239.

Chapter Six: With Vision

1. Peter Marshall, quoted in *12,000 Religious Quotations*, Frank S. Mead, ed. (Grand Rapids: Baker, 1989), 465.

2. John Stott, *Involvement: Social and Sexual Relationships in the Modern World*, vol. 2 (Old Tappan, N.J.: Fleming H. Revell, 1985), 147.

3. Ibid., 148, 156.

4. Gien Karssen, *Her Name Is Woman*, bk. 2 (Colorado Springs: NavPress, 1977), 89.

5. Edith Deen, *Family Living in the Bible* (New York: Harper & Row, 1963), 82.

6. Hannah More, *Religion of the Heart*, Hal M. Helms, ed. (Orleans, Mass.: Paraclete Press, 1993), ix.

7. Marianne Thornton, quoted in K. Moore, *She for God* (London: Allison and Busby, 1978), 136.

8. Hannah More, *The Complete Works of Hannah More*, vol. 1 (New York: Derby, 1856), 446.

9. Samuel Johnson, quoted in More, *Religion of the Heart*, ix.

10. Hannah More, *The Letters of Hannah More* (London: John Lane, The Bodley Head, 1925), 20–21.

11. William Wilberforce, *Real Christianity*, James M. Houston, ed. (Portland, Ore.: Multnomah, 1982), xii.

12. Thomas Price, *Memoir of Wilberforce* (Boston: Light & Stearns, 1836), 11.

13. Ernest Marshall Howse, *Saints in Politics* (Toronto: University of Toronto, 1952), vii.

14. Ibid., 26.

15. Elie Halévy, *History of the English People in 1815* (London: n.p., 1926), 381.

16. More, "Cultivating a Devotional Spirit," *Religion of the Heart*, 63.

17. Jeremy and Margaret Collingwood, *Hannah More* (Oxford: Lion, 1990), 57–58.

18. Jill Evans, *Beloved and Chosen* (Norwich, Norfolk, Great Britain: Canterbury Press, 1993), 159.

19. Hannah More, quoted in *12,000 Religious Quotations*, Mead, 135.

20. Collingwood, *Hannah More*, 7–8.

21. More, *Complete Works*, 438.

22. Hannah More, "Self-Love," in *Spiritual Awakening*, Sherwood Eliot Wirt, ed. (Westchester, Ill.: Crossway, 1986), 75–76.

23. More, *Complete Works*, 451.

24. John Lord, quoted in Edith Deen, *Great Women of the Christian Faith*, (Uhrichsville, Ohio: Barbour, reprinted by arrangement with Harper & Row, 1959), 355.

25. Dietrich Bonhoeffer, *The Cost of Discipleship* (New York: Macmillan, 1963), 192.

26. Ibid, 192–93.

27. Oswald Chambers, *My Utmost for His Highest* (New York: Dodd, Mead, 1935), 364.

Bibliography

Adels, Jill Haak, ed. *The Wisdom of the Saints*. New York: Oxford University Press, 1987.

Arnold, Duane W. H., trans. *Prayers of the Martyrs*. Grand Rapids: Zondervan, 1991.

Attwater, Donald. *The Avenel Dictionary of Saints*. New York: Avenel, 1965.

Bartlett, John. *Familiar Quotations*, 15th ed. Boston: Little, Brown, 1980.

Beckett, Wendy. *Sister Wendy's Book of Saints*. London: Dorling Kindersley, 1998.

Bede. *A History of the English Church and Its People*. London: Penguin Classics, 1955.

Berry, Jo. *The Priscilla Principle*. Grand Rapids: Zondervan, 1984.

Bonhoeffer, Dietrich. *The Cost of Discipleship*. New York: Macmillan, 1963.

_____. *The Mystery of Holy Night*. New York: Crossroad, 1996.

Brandt, Keith. *Rosa Parks*. New York: Troll Communications, 1993.

Brown, R. Lamon. *Growing Spiritually with the Saints: Catherine of Genoa & William Law*. Macon, Ga.: Peake Road, 1996.

Buechner, Frederick. *Wishful Thinking*. New York: Harper & Row, 1973.

Butler, Alban. *Lives of the Saints*. New York: Barnes & Noble, 1997.

Cahill, Thomas. *How the Irish Saved Civilization*. New York: Anchor/Doubleday, 1995.

Carlson, Margaret. *Grace Grows Best in Winter*. Grand Rapids: Eerdmans, 1984.

Carmichael, Amy. *Whispers of His Power*. Old Tappan, N.J.: Fleming H. Revell, 1982.

Catherine of Genoa. *The Spiritual Dialogue*, trans. Serge Hughes. Mahwah, N.J.: Paulist Press, 1979.

Caussade, Jean-Pierre de. *Self-Abandonment to Divine Providence*. Springfield, Ill.: Templegate, 1959.

_____. *Spiritual Letters of Jean-Pierre de Caussade*, trans. Kitty Muggeridge. Wilton, Conn.: Morehouse-Barlow, 1986.

Chambers, Oswald. *My Utmost for His Highest*. New York: Dodd, Mead, 1935.

Chenu, Bruno et al. *The Book of Christian Martyrs*. New York: Crossroad, 1990.

Clarkson, Margaret. *Grace Grows Best in Winter*. Grand Rapids: Eerdmans, 1984.

Classics Devotional Bible, The. Grand Rapids: Zondervan, 1996.

Collingwood, Jeremy and Margaret. *Hannah More*. Oxford: Lion, 1990.

Colson, Charles. *Loving God*. Grand Rapids: Zondervan, 1983.

Cowan, Tom. *The Way of the Saints*. New York: G. P. Putnam's, 1998.

Deen, Edith. *All of the Women of the Bible*. San Francisco: Harper, 1955.

_____. *Family Living in the Bible*. New York: Harper & Row, 1963.

_____. *Great Women of the Christian Faith*. Uhrichsville, Ohio: Barbour, reprinted by arrangement with Harper & Row, 1959.

Dictionary of Saints. London: Brockhampton Press, 1996.

Dowley, Tim, ed. *Eerdmans Handbook to the History of Christianity*. Grand Rapids: Eerdmans, 1977.

Downey, Michael. *Trappist: Living in the Land of Desire*. New York: Paulist Press, 1997.

Eisen, Armand, ed. *On Being Christian*. Kansas City: Ariel/Andrews and McMeel, 1995.

Elliot, Elisabeth. *Gateway to Joy*. Ann Arbor, Mich.: Servant, 1998.

_____. *These Strange Ashes*. New York: Harper & Row, 1975.

Ellsberg, Robert. *All Saints*. New York: Crossroad, 1997.

Engelbert, Omer. *The Lives of the Saints*. New York: Barnes & Noble, 1994.

Evans, Jill. *Beloved and Chosen*. Norwich, Norfolk, Great Britain: Canterbury Press, 1993.

Farmer, David Hugh. *The Oxford Dictionary of Saints*, 3rd. ed. Oxford: Oxford University Press, 1992.

Foster, Richard J. *Prayer: Finding the Heart's True Home*. San Francisco: Harper-Collins, 1992.

_____. *Prayers from the Heart*. San Francisco: Harper, 1994.

Foster, Richard J. and James Bryan Smith, eds. *Devotional Classics*. San Francisco: Harper, 1990.

Fox's Book of Martyrs. New York: William L. Allison, 1890.

Garvin, Paul, trans. and ed. *The Life and Sayings of St. Catherine of Genoa*. Staten Island, N.Y.: Alba, 1964.

Halévy, Elie. *History of the English People in 1815*. London: n.p., 1926.

Hammarskjöld, Dag. *Markings*. New York: Alfred A. Knopf, 1970.

Hillby, Carolyn Miles, ed. *The World's Great Religious Poetry*. New York: Macmillan, 1923.

Howse, Ernest Marshall. *Saints in Politics*. Toronto: University of Toronto, 1952.

Hudson, Robert R. and Shelley Townsend-Hudson, eds. *Companions for the Soul*. Grand Rapids: Zondervan, 1995.

Hügel, Frederich von. *The Mystical Element of Religion As Studied in Saint Catherine of Genoa and Her Friends*, vol. 1. London: J. M. Dent, 1908.

Jones, Alison. *Saints*. Edinburgh: Chambers, 1992.

Karssen, Gien. *Her Name Is Woman*, bk. 1. Colorado Springs: NavPress, 1975.

_____. *Her Name Is Woman*, bk. 2. Colorado Springs: NavPress, 1977.

Kepler, Thomas S. *A Journey with the Saint*. Cleveland: World, 1951.

Keyes, Dick. *Beyond Identity: Finding Your Self in the Image and Character of God*. Ann Arbor, Mich.: Servant, 1984.

Lewis, C. S. *The Four Loves*. London: Geoffrey Bles, 1960.

_____. *George MacDonald: An Anthology*. London: Fount, 1983.

_____. *Mere Christianity*. New York: Macmillan, 1960.

Life and Doctrine of Saint Catherine of Genoa, The. New York: Catholic Publication Society, 1874.

Lindbergh, Anne Morrow. *Gift from the Sea*. New York: Random House, 1975.

Llewelyn, Robert, ed. *The Joy of the Saints*. Springfield, Ill.: Templegate, 1988.

Loxton, Howard. *The Encyclopedia of Saints.* Stamford, Conn.: Longmeadow, 1996.

Macartney, Clarence Edward. *Great Women of the Bible.* Grand Rapids: Kregel, 1991.

MacDonald, George. *A Hidden Life and Other Poems.* New York: Scribner, Armstrong, 1872.

Matheson, George. *Portraits of Bible Women.* Grand Rapids: Kregel, 1987.

Matthews, Victor H. *Manners and Customs in Bible Times.* Peabody, Mass.: Hendrickson, 1988.

McGinley, Phyllis. *Saint Watching.* New York: Crossroad, 1989.

Mead, Frank S., ed. *12,000 Religious Quotations.* Grand Rapids: Baker, 1989.

Michener, James. *The Source.* New York: Random House, 1965.

Moore, K. *She for God.* London: Allison and Busby, 1978.

More, Hannah. *The Complete Works of Hannah More,* vol. 1. New York: Derby, 1856.

_____. *The Letters of Hannah More.* London: John Lane, The Bodley Head, 1925.

_____. *Religion of the Heart.,* ed. Hal M. Helms. Orleans, Mass.: Paraclete Press, 1993.

Morgan, Tom. *Saints.* San Francisco: Chronicle, 1994.

Murray, Andrew. *Abide in Christ.* Old Tappan, N.J.: Spire/Fleming H. Revell, n.d.

Mursurillo, Herbert. *The Acts of the Christian Martyrs.* Oxford: Clarendon, 1972.

Norris, Kathleen. *Cloister Walk.* New York: Riverhead, 1996.

Oden, Amy, ed. *In Her Own Words: Women's Writings in the History of Christian Thought.* Nashville: Abingdon, 1994.

Owens, Virginia Stem. *Daughters of Eve.* Colorado Springs: NavPress, 1995.

Packer, J. I. *Knowing God.* Downers Grove, Ill.: InterVarsity Press, 1973.

Parks, Rosa. *Quiet Strength.* Grand Rapids: Zondervan, 1994.

Patterson, Ben. *Waiting: Finding Hope When God Seems Silent.* Downers Grove, Ill.: InterVarsity Press, 1989.

Peterson, Eugene H. *A Long Obedience in the Same Direction.* Downers Grove, Ill.: InterVarsity Press, 1980.

Price, Thomas. *Memoir of Wilberforce.* Boston: Light & Stearns, 1836.

Roche, Lissa, ed. *The Christian's Treasury.* Westchester, Ill.: Crossway, 1995.

Rossetti, Christina. *Goblin Market and Other Poems.* London: Macmillan, 1862.

Shelley, Bruce. *All the Saints Adore Thee.* Grand Rapids: Baker, 1988.

Stott, John. *Involvement: Social and Sexual Relationships in the Modern World,* vol. 2. Old Tappan, N.J.: Fleming H. Revell, 1985.

Sykes, William, ed. *Visions of Faith.* Basingstoke, England: Marshall Pickering, 1986.

Temple, William. *Christ in His Church.* London: Macmillan, 1925.

Toon, Peter. *Spiritual Companions: An Introduction to the Christian Classics.* Grand Rapids: Baker, 1990.

Topping, Eva Catafygiotu. *Saints and Sisterhood: The Lives of Forty-Eight Holy Women.* Minneapolis: Life and Light, 1990.

Tozer, A. W. *The Knowledge of the Holy.* New York: Harper & Row, 1961.

_____. *The Pursuit of God*. Camp Hill, Penn.: Christian Publications, 1982.

Trueblood, Elton. *The Company of the Committed*. New York: Harper & Row, 1961.

Tucker, Ruth A. and Walter Liefeld, *Daughters of the Church*. Grand Rapids: Zondervan, 1987.

Walsh, Michael, ed. *Butler's Lives of the Saints*. San Francisco: Harper, 1991.

Walsh, Sheila. *Bring Back the Joy*. Grand Rapids: Zondervan, 1998.

Ward, Benedicta, ed. *Daily Readings with the Desert Fathers*. Springfield, Ill.: Templegate, 1990.

Ward, Hannah and Jennifer Wild, compilers. *The Doubleday Christian Quotation Collection*. New York: Doubleday, 1997.

White, John. *The Fight*. Downers Grove, Ill.: InterVarsity Press, 1976.

White, Kristin E. *A Guide to the Saints*. New York: Ballantine, 1991.

Wilberforce, William. *Real Christianity*, ed. James M. Houston. Portland, Ore.: Multnomah Press, 1982.

Wilson-Kastner, Patricia. *A Lost Tradition: Women Writers of the Early Church*. Lanham, N.Y.: University Press of America, 1981.

Wirt, Sherwood Eliot, ed. *Spiritual Awakening*. Westchester, Ill.: Crossway, 1986.

Wright, Elliott. *Holy Company: Christian Heroes and Heroines*. New York: Macmillan, 1980.

Women
of
Character

Debra Evans

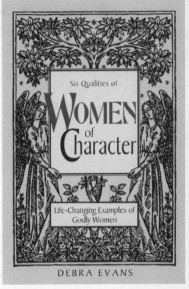

Today's Christian woman longs for role models who can help shape a life of purpose, depth, and value. Debra Evans introduces a dozen biblical and historical figures whose lives exemplify six life-changing character traits of a godly woman: brokenness, belief, surrender, obedience, devotion, and service. And though their stories span centuries, the message is relevant today.

Women of Character weaves prayers, interviews with contemporary women, and classic writings with remarkable tales of empowerment, focus, and meaningful living. These uplifting accounts will inspire you to find your own place among "the company of heaven."

**Pick up your copy at your favorite
Christian bookstore today!**

Softcover 0-310-21921-3

We want to hear from you. Please send your comments about this book to us in care of the address below. Thank you.

ZondervanPublishingHouse

Grand Rapids, Michigan 49530

http://www.zondervan.com